MILITANT ISLAM IN AMERICA

Also by Marshall Frank

BEYOND THE CALL

DIRE STRAITS

FRANKLY SPEAKING

ON MY FATHER'S GRAVE

CALL ME MOMMY

THE LATENT: A MIAMI NOVEL

MILITANT ISLAM IN AMERICA

Brutally Frank Series: Vol. 1

Marshall Frank

FORTIS BOOKS

Fortis Books
182 Howard Street
unit 427
San Francisco, Ca. 94105-1611
Fortis10@gmail.com

SAN: 851 - 3694

Copyright (c) 2006 by Marshall Frank
ISBN-13: 978-0-9718709-0-1
ISBN-10: 0-9718709-0-X

Cover design by Aude Metz

First Fortis Books printing: July 2006

Printed in the U.S.A.

TABLE OF CONTENTS

PREFACE

On September 11th, 2001, I was at 31,000 feet aboard a British Airways flight from London to Charlotte, busily writing notes for a new article, when the captain announced over the public address that our plane was being diverted to Moncton, New Brunswick. He said that a commercial airliner had smashed into the World Trade Center, and all U.S. airports were being closed. After a two-hour stand-by on the tarmac of this remote township (which I'd never heard of) all passengers were shuffled off to a hockey coliseum which would become our home for the next three days, and the home for 2,500 passengers of twenty-two other diverted flights as well.

When the bus pulled up, I looked out the window and saw chaos. Red Cross volunteers scurried about as they set up stations, phones and tables. People were running around in circles, creating a sense of uneasiness among the passengers. Once inside, I glanced up at the huge television monitor and watched, for the first time, the grisly image of commercial airplanes ramming into the giant edifice. The tape repeated itself over and over, with an inserted photo of a bearded man in the upper right corner, a man I'd never heard of: Osama bin Laden. I was amazed at how soon the news media identified the culprit behind the attacks, as though his fingerprints were instantly found all over the walls of the 110 story towers.

As I stared at the giant TV screen, I thought about the terror that raged in the hearts and minds of innocent travelers aboard those planes before they were all incinerated.

I thought about the horror that ravaged the minds of people in the upper floors of the World Trade Center. One minute, they were comfortably at work. In an instant, they were forced to decide if they would die by fire or by jumping a thousand feet to the street below.

I thought about the citizens of New York City who, for the first time in nearly two hundred years, were witness to a wartime attack inside the shores of our heretofore invulnerable nation.

I thought about the struggle aboard United Airlines Flight 93, that was headed to the nation's capitol, but somehow crashed in a Pennsylvania field, killing forty-five instead of one thousand or more.

I thought about our impenetrable Pentagon, the fortress of our Defense Department, and how it was essentially defenseless to the plan of attack by rogue aliens.

The German Nazis couldn't do it. The Japs never got closer than Pearl Harbor. Viet Nam was a debacle, but it took place half way around the world.

It was a day that would change millions of lives, more than we would realize. It put complacent Americans on notice, that we were no longer immune from invasion, from global hate and from an insurgency that could bring down the most powerful country in the world. It was no longer a detached television image on CNN taking place in a foreign land. It was here. Chills ran up and down my body, knowing how easy it was for fanatics to plan and execute a mass slaughter that would end the lives of 3,000 people in four carefully coordinated events one day inside our borders. That's just shy of the number of men killed in battle during the entire Revolutionary War.

But numbers don't really tell the story, because that one-day massacre resulted in the killing of one person multiplied 3,000 times over. Each and every victim had a productive life, filled with love and dreams, all smashed in one terrorizing event, and leaving five and ten times that many grieving with broken hearts that can never be repaired.

Just as in natural disasters, war and major accidents, death-toll numbers tend to cloud the enormity of the loss. Stalin once said, "*One death is a tragedy. A thousand deaths is a statistic.*"

Since retiring from a thirty-year law enforcement career in 1990, I've been writing novels and newspaper articles about a myriad of topics. Many of my police compatriots think I'm a bleeding heart liberal because I favor abolishment of capital punishment and decriminalization of many drug laws. I've also written about religious freedom, and how it applies to all Americans not just Christians, which make up the overwhelming majority. I've stood up for Jews, Pagans, atheists, and Muslims because I feel it vitally important that all religions, and non-religions be protected from governmental intrusion. We are all free to practice whatever religion we choose while free, as well, from religious coercion.

My impression of Muslims was like most Americans, just another religion. They revere

Muhammad like Christians revere Jesus. They have a Quran, Christians have a Bible and Jews have a Torah. They worship in mosques, others worship in synagogues and churches. It was all like an equal playing field, all about love and goodness, with slight differences in approach.

I knew about the first World Trade Center bombing. I knew about The U.S.S. Cole. I knew about all the other thousands of terrorist murders that had taken place around the world in the past forty years, a la Islamic fanaticism. But I figured, like most, that this was the product of an extremist faction that did not represent the majority of Muslims around the world, and that Islam was basically a religion of peace, as told to us by our president and other leaders world wide.

I was wrong.

So is the president.

It's important to know one's enemy. After all, knowledge, they say, is power. The enemy certainly knows us.

After 9/11, I began researching Islam, bearing in mind that this is a religion that guides over one billion people in the world. I wanted to remain as neutral as possible, and absorb the writings of pro-Islamists as well as anti-Islamists. I embarked on selected readings inside the Quran as well. Somewhere along the line, I read an article about a columnist's research into a number of mosques inside the United Sates that were allegedly preaching hate and future insurgency to thousands of small children. I wondered, just how true this was, and if it posed a viable threat to the future of our nation. I then probed into Islam further reading and absorbing as much as possible, knowing I would be writing about this one day, to inform the American people.

Some may ask, what makes me an expert? I am definitely not an expert. Before anything else, I am an American and a lifelong student of crime and security. I am also a career police professional with — I believe — an ample supply of common sense. Like many of my readers, I love my country and fear for its future. I'm just one of those who has pulled my head from the proverbial sand and tuned in to the world's serious problems.

What knowledge I've acquired, any American can acquire. The information is out there for the seeking. It's a matter of retrieving from the internet, at the library, at book stores, at lectures and then studying like one would study for a master's thesis.

Many renowned journalists and syndicated columnists from all sides of the spectrum have researched and written about this problem, including Michele Malkin, Cal Thomas, Michael Savage, Suzanne Fields, Molly Ivins, Bill O'Reilly, Carl Hiaasen, Paul Greenberg, Frank Gaffney and more. Numerous books have been published on the subject, some of which were used as reference for these chapters. They include: *The Islamization of America,* by Abdullah Al-Araby, *Holy War On The Home Front,* by Harvey Kushner, *Inside The Kingdom,* by Carmen Bin Laden, *The History Of Islam,* by Robert Payne, *The Infidels,* by David Anderson, *A History of Islamic Societies,* by Ira M. Lapidus, *The Politically Incorrect Guide to Islam,* by Robert Spencer, *Infiltration,* by Paul Sperry, *The Professors,* by David Horowitz, *The Prophet Of Doom,* by Craig Winn, and *Taking Back Islam: American Muslims Reclaim Their Faith,* edited by

Michael Wolf.

Many will see my background only as a career cop and retired homicide detective with questionable credentials for writing these startling revelations. Therefore it's important for the reader to know my sources.

What I impart in *Brutally Frank: Militant Islam in America*, is nothing other than an easy-to-read summation of facts and conditions already known to the well-informed, plus a few hard-nosed opinions thrown in for impact. Anyone who delves into the truth will be as shocked as I was to learn what is really happening throughout the world, and inside our country today. Our government representatives have failed us miserably in this regard.

What I've discovered completely shattered my view of Islam, and all it stands for. Particularly the militant side. Yes, it is a peaceful religion, so long as everyone complies with the edicts of Islam. For those who are consider infidels (non-believers), it is not so peaceful, especially where Muslims are in control.

The book is intended to be forthright and honest without ambiguity. I wish not to complicate issues with arrays of statistics, dates, quotations, and smokescreens so thick, it's difficult to understand what we're talking about. The purpose of this book is to boil it all down to simple English. Here is the crux: World War III is here. It's not in Iraq, it's not in North Korea, or Iran and Syria. It's everywhere, including Africa, Europe and most chillingly, inside the borders of the United States. And it's being waged on two fronts, one we can see, and the other we can't... or refuse to.

We can see al Qaeda and it's brand of terror every day on news reports. We know about death tolls, suicide bombings, political rhetoric, and what the media and the government carefully scripts what they want us to know. We know a lot of this because it makes sensational news. What people don't see, does not make sensational news. What most Americans don't see is the surreptitious infiltration of our enemy from within, viciously designed to take over our way of life. It's happening right now, like a cancer rooting into the deepest cells of our nation, then spreading throughout the body until it is finally dead.

War Of The Worlds, a Steven Spielberg film released in 2005, tells the story of aliens who furtively invaded the United States and lay patiently dormant in the subterranean underworld for many years until the time to invade was ripe. When the power and resources were finally in place, and the people were complacent, the aliens emerged from within causing havoc and revolution, catching the nation by surprise. It was all part of the grand plan, not much different than what is going on today. In fact, 9/11 was nothing less than a clandestine invasion by patient insurgents hellbent on mass murder, and they succeeded.

In the movie plot, unlike today's world, no one saw it coming. In the world of 2006, the signs are everywhere, but we — and the government — refuse to acknowledge what is in front of our very noses.

Before we can effectively address the issue of our nation's security and the advent of World War III, we must first identify our most serious threat: Militant Islam. Bear in mind, "militant Islam" is not a minor little splinter group out of the mainstream of that religion, like James Jones was to Christianity, or Timothy McVeigh was to American militia.

Militant Islam is huge. It's international. Led by the combined efforts of Osama Bin Laden's Al Qaeda network plus Saudi Arabia and their Wahhabi form of Islam, it spans more than forty nations comprising millions upon millions of people who are psychologically and spiritually programmed to hate the west. It is an ominous threat to be reckoned with, here and abroad.

Millions of Muslims around the world — including those who are not "militant" — have been taught to hate Jews, Christians, Americans, and infidels in general, in that order. It has nothing to do with economic depravity or ethnic prejudice, as some sympathizers would have us believe. The hate is simply inbred. It's in integral part of the culture, and the religion. Children of Muslims are indoctrinated from birth to know and understand no other way of life, then they grow to indoctrinate the next generation. They are multiplying, world wide, by the billions.

In truth, this is nothing so covert that we can't see it. We just refuse to. Comatose Americans are generally open minded and think about Islam as though it were just another faith, like Judaism, Christianity, Buddhism, Shinto, and so forth. But it is not. It is a form of government based on religious premise, designed to control people's lives, every day, every moment, from birth to death.

Hundreds of journalists and government officials have written about it, exposed it, and told us what's happening. But if Americans don't personally experience a suicide bomber, see those dead bodies strewn around a train station, or smell the blood or feel the loss, we don't believe it's happening to us. It's happening to strangers 10,000 miles away, and we go about our daily lives unaffected. We, inside the United States, are not paying attention. I often ask people if they have studied the Islamic issue internationally and inside America. Those who have, are a rarity. Average Americans face issues on a need-to-know basis, our minds in the present, and the future be damned. We really don't care what conditions our grandchildren will live under, so long as we take care of ourselves and our kids, today. We are happy and secure inside our homes, counting our investments, watching CNN or home movies, playing with computers and eating at restaurants, going about our daily lives thinking that Mr. Bush and Karl Rove is taking care of the international terror problem by waging war in Iraq. It really doesn't faze us, other than a few news stories now and then, and perhaps, a bump in the economy, and a few lives lost overseas. In fact, we are blind to the obvious around us.

Americans have become inured to often-heard phrases proffered by media and politicians, like the "War On Drugs." "The War on Poverty." "Fighting for Freedom." And, of course, "The War on Terror." After a while, they are so redundant, it's in one ear and out the other. Refusing to face up to the true enemy, as we did in past wars, could portend the end of us, as we know it. We fail to focus on the sinister war taking place on this side of the Atlantic. It is a war that cannot be compared to World War I and II, nor Korea, or even Viet Nam. It's a war against a wide-spread ideology that has no battle lines. The enemy has no uniforms and no country. The playing field is inside of our own skin and minds. It's a war going on right inside our borders today, a war the enemy is plotting, executing and — so far — winning.

It is a war that will bring the United States to its knees in the next fifty years, or less. Yet, we continue on with a conventional conflict in a foreign land, with guns and tanks, as though we were still fighting Nazi Germany. I wonder if that's not what al Qaeda had in mind all along, lure our military and $500 billion dollars in commitment 10,000 miles away, while America is infiltrated and converted from within.

The Bush administration would serve the people well by boldly declaring who we are at war with, not the ambiguous term, "terror." Terror, is a condition. Terror is an emotion. We are not at war with an emotion, we are at war with crazed fanatics who practice a way of life that represent a billion people throughout the world. They are a determined people, driven by faith, and they are well financed, much of it from a boomerang of American dollars .

We are at war with militant Islam.

The national government know that. So why aren't they being honest with us?

Our politically correct president remains ever cautious to avoid offending Islamics. Rather, he refers to our enemy as terrorists and insurgents, which avoids any mention of the infiltrators. Yet, many clerics, and other Islamic leaders have openly declared their goal to eventually rename our land, the "Islamic Republic Of America." They've announced it on American soil, with the full knowledge of our government. They've done the same in Europe.

Our government's response? We must be politically correct. Americans are told we are only at war with terrorists. At the same time, we are told that Islam is a peaceful religion, leading us to believe that it's only the active terrorists who we should fear.

Meanwhile, the president has hosted numerous Muslim clerics as honored guests at the White House who were later indicted and/or deported for supporting terrorist activity. And the Bush family remains, to this day, warm and cozy with the royal Saudi family.

Until we are willing to identify the enemy, there is no hope of defeating them. The end result, will be: burkas, beheadings, religious police and Islamic rule.

We can't afford to not believe it.

There are some who will accuse me of being racist, bigoted and intolerant of other cultures and religions. I will vehemently deny those labels to my dying day. I love all peoples of the world, but not unconditionally. I'm no Jesus. I do not love my enemies. Those who seek harm for me, my family and friends, and my great country, I hold anger, animosity and fear.

Some who have read my articles say I am a fear monger. I rather think of myself as a pragmatist trying to alert people of an ominous and deadly threat that is looming for us all. In the 1920's and 30's, many pragmatists saw what was coming in Europe but the pacifists called them fear mongers. Had the world listened to the so-called "fear mongers", we may have averted a war that took over 50 million lives.

This book will tell it like it is and what we can do about it, not as our government or Islamic sympathizers would have us believe. This book is based on stark reality. It is not politically correct. It is, in fact, Brutally Frank.

"For years, 'Mein Kampf' stood as proof of the blindness and complacency of the world. For in its pages, Hitler announced — long before he came to power — a program of blood and terror in a self-revelation of such overwhelming frankness that few among its readers had the courage to believe it."
— Konrad Heiden, author of *Der Feuhrer*

CHAPTER ONE

THE PEACEFUL RELIGION

"Fight those who do not believe in Allah, nor in the latter day, nor do they prohibit what Allah and His Apostle have prohibited, nor follow the religion of truth, out of those who have been given the Book, until they pay the tax in acknowledgment of superiority and they are in a state of subjection."
—From the Quran. Surah 9:29

Boiled down, Surah 9:29 tells us that peace is reserved for Muslims and all those who are not Muslims shall pay for protection. In my law enforcement career, we called that extortion. And, if protection is not paid, what be the consequence?

It's interesting to note that the term, "Islam," means submission, not peace as some would have us believe.

Islam certainly is a peaceful religion, so long as you are a devout compliant Muslim, and not deemed an infidel.

Infidels are non-believers. That is, people who do not accept Islam and Allah as their God. That means, Jews, Christians, Buddhists, Atheists and all non-Muslims, are infidels. They, in a nutshell, are the targets for the soldiers of jihad.

Though several and varied definitions exist, depending on whose perspective one wishes to adopt, the basic meaning of jihad can be pared down to simple terms. Jihad is holy war. It means the compulsory and communal effort to expand territories ruled by Muslims at the expense of territories presently ruled by non-Muslims. The purpose of jihad, in other words, is to extend sovereign Muslim power with the eventual goal of achieving Muslim dominion over the entire planet. Terrorism is but one method to achieve this goal. There are others, less visible, but just as sinister, and just as effective. Regardless of the methods employed, their end justifies whatever means they employ, whether it be violence, deception, infiltration, espionage and the exploitation of rights intended to protect Americans. In reality, those rights are now protecting our enemies.

I believe that knowledge begets power, and ignorance begets vulnerability. The sooner America educates themselves to the threat, and exercises their power through public outcry and at the polls, the sooner we can meet and repel the enemy. If we don't, it may soon be too late. We must do three things: We must become educated, we must think and we must reject complacency.

We hear a lot of rhetoric about tolerance. Tolerance is a glowing term, which — in most cases — we certainly should employ when it comes to ethnic, racial and religious diversity. But tolerance of an avowed and formidable enemy who hides behind the shield of religion is pure lunacy. Would we have shown tolerance to the American Nazis in 1944?

In most militant Muslim societies, Islam is as much a form of government as it is a religion. In fact, it is both. In strict mid-east Islamic nations, the two cannot be separated. Militant Islamics have openly announced their intent to replace our constitution with the Quran. Consequently, this is not a religion to be compared in parallel with Christianity or Judaism. It is a way of governing people much the same as it was in Nazi Germany or the Soviet Union. The difference: No borders. No uniforms. There can be no regime change because the head of government is unseen: Allah.

Most would agree, that anyone who is interested in learning about Christianity should study the life and times of Jesus. Buddhists know of Buddha, Jews of Moses, and so forth. Likewise, to learn about Islam, one must study the life and times of its founder, Muhammad. After all, had there not been a Muhammad, there would not have been Islam.

During my probe into the life of the prophet, I had expected to learn about a Christ-like figure, a sinless man much like Jesus or Mahatma Gandhi who preached nothing but love, peace and goodness for all. After all, he started up a religion that now guides over a billion people. What I learned was nothing of the sort.

Biographies of Muhammad abound. Though the basics about his life are generally in accord, interpretations are slanted depending on which side of the orientation scale one views from. Devout Muslims disregard anything that sounds negative because they are taught to believe what they wish to believe, regardless of historical evidence. More neutral students of Muhammad write from a critical perspective. There are few biographies, or hadith (stories about the life of the prophet) that were written by people who lived in his time, other than himself. Two of them were Abu Dawud and Sahih Bukhari. Much that is written about Muhammad comes from these sources. More is known about the complete life of Muhammad, than we ever knew about Jesus.

Born in 571 A. D., Muhammad lost his mother and father before the age of six and was raised in Mecca by his uncle who would often take him on trading journeys to Syria. Through this, he became an able merchant, familiar with foreign ways. And, he was, without doubt, a peaceful man. When Muhammad was 25 years of age he married Khadijah, a rich employer fifteen years his elder. She bore five children. She died 24 years later, leaving him quite wealthy.

It appears that this gentleman from Mecca lived an unassuming life until the age of forty when, in 610, he experienced a vision of the angel Gabriel while meditating in a cave. Then he heard a voice, assumed to be from Allah. "You are the Messenger of God." The voice told him to recite Quran, which means, recitation. This was the beginning of Islam as the prophet was divinely dispatched to spread the one-God message to his people, to guide, to instruct and institute laws of behavior. Now certain that he was an apostle, Muhammad returned to embrace the voice many times over the years and follow the instructions of Allah, from which he was destined to spread His word.

After Muhammad established his new religion, he gained a small number of followers but had a tough time convincing the masses that he was truly God's messenger. It was the will of Allah that he convert as many as possible to Islamic thought. After thirteen years without much luck, he resettled from Mecca to Medina in 622, where he took on a new tactic for converting people: The sword. No one knows, for sure, what triggered the sudden change in his approach to converting people, but it sure proved that violence succeeded where peace did not.

As followers grew into armies, people converted for three reasons. First, fear. Second, because they became convinced of Muhammad's link to God. Third, to reap the benefits of belonging to the new order. From there, Muhammad became emboldened by a sense of godliness and power, and sought to gain more followers. But they were far and few between, especially among the Christians and the Jews. The Jews, in particular, were resistant to conversion, a perplexing problem to the prophet.

After the death of Khadijah, Muhammad went on to marry between nine and thirteen women, depending on whose history one wishes to accept. One of those was a six year old girl, Aisha, with whom he did not consummate the marriage until she was nine. I found that a baffling revelation. Translated, "consummate" means, he waited until she was nine to have sex with her. This, the holy man.

Imagine Jesus having sexual intercourse with a nine-year-old girl?

Starting in 622, Muhammad's army of followers engaged in raiding parties against Meccan caravans, from which they reaped the spoils. They justified the killing of innocent people because they were non-believers, and therefore, not innocent. Muhammad then conquered a number of surrounding tribes, converting people to Islam lest they be killed. Having won a number of battles and skirmishes against the forces of Mecca, he became more emboldened. People saw him as a great leader, a prophet and an apostle of God. And that's how he saw himself. But as gentle he was as a man during his early years, he was just as brutal during his conquering years.

One gruesome example was the aftermath of the Battle of the Trench in 627. In order to withstand another attack from the Meccans, the forces within Medina dug a wide trench around the city. The armies traded insults over the trench, but the attacking army withdrew after two weeks leaving few casualties. It was a great victory for Muhammad. But he was disturbed over learning that some of the Jews in the city remained neutral, and did not wholly support his new order. After all, Jews have a way of wanting to remain Jewish. Shortly thereafter, with Allah's blessing, around 600 Jewish men were lined up before the city's inhabitants, marched/dragged in groups of six or seven and ceremoniously beheaded, alive, one by one, their bodies thrown into the trench. One can barely visualize the horror of those images, the screams of the condemned, blood squirting like geysers from the carotid artery, carcases flopping into the trench, Muslims shouting and cheering, non-Muslims weeping and petrified, and Muhammad sitting upon a camel or horse, watching, approving, declaring this to be the will of Allah.

Their wives and children were sold as slaves. Muhammad took one of those wives and made her his concubine.

If that didn't make converts out of the remaining non-believers, nothing would. I bear these things in mind when I hear how 1.2 billion people subscribe to the peaceful religion.

All of this was recorded in the Hadith by Bukhari.

Beheadings are still practiced by the government of Saudi Arabia in 2006. They are also practiced by al Qaeda around the world.

In 630 A.D., after eight years of violent conflict, the apostle of peace rode into Mecca with 10,000 men and captured his city of birth without resistence. Islam theocracy was thereby established and all the people of the region committed to the new religion.

Before his death from natural causes in 632 A.D., Muhammad had established Islam as a religious, social and political force throughout most of Arabia. With unity restored, and following the command of Muhammad to spread Islam throughout the world, the now-powerful Muslims looked outward and commenced conquests that would eventually bond all of the mid-east, and far away nations into the grasp of the new religion.

Imagine, for one moment: You are a peaceful man living in the Tunisian desert, c. 645 A.D., with your family of one wife and five children, knowing little or nothing about the world outside your immediate domain. One morning, you're surprised to see two thousand strange men on horses and camels galloping over the desert horizon, wielding swords, thundering through your village, and declaring dominance at the will of Allah. They tell you to submit and convert to Islam. The first few people who refuse, are beheaded on the spot. You look over to your children. What do you do? Now, multiply your situation by the millions.

Such tells the story of how the "religion of peace" spread across the world. The roots took hold in Arabia. The growth of the tree of Islam and it's branches grew far and wide with resistence now and then that erupted into wars and battles, heralded as heroic events in the Islamic calendar. But have no doubt, these were pre-emptive invasions of villages and nations by a brutal army hellbent on global control, justified by the will of Allah. (Sound familiar?) From Arabia, the Muslims conquered Syria, then Egypt, Iran, Jerusalem and eventually dominating the entire mid-east, North Africa and all of Spain by the year 711 A.D. They met their first major defeat at Paris in 733, which seems to have cooled their heels for a few centuries. Later, they went on to conquer Turkey where they established the Ottoman Empire in the 14th century. They were driven back from Vienna in the 18th century. But the same pattern never changes, regardless of what century, what country, or what barriers they face. It's the wish of Allah, they say, and the duty of all Muslims — one way or another — to make that happen. That is their priority, before anything, anyone, cr any government. We should never lose sight of that.

Some defenders of the Islamic way will refer to these historical men as "brave warriors", but let's be honest. When an army invades a peaceful community and begins killing innocent people, that's called murder. And it scares the hell out of those left alive, who want to save their necks.

By all accounts of history, and by witnessing the horrible events that have taken place throughout the world today, we Americans, and all the people within free nations should have no illusions. Militant Islam's main goal is world conquest, and has been — without wavering — for 1400 years. Just like in the seventh century, power and control is assumed through murder and mayhem. Muslims such as Osama Bin Laden will not rest until they see all the world — including America — under Islamic rule. It is their goal to see all women suffer life inside a burka. It is their goal that every nation kneels to the call for prayer five times a day. It is their goal to have us all revert to a life of seventh century primitives. Not much different than the Nazis, it is their goal to annihilate all Jews, only without the ovens. It is their goal that people of all lands worship Allah, lest they are killed. This is not an empty threat. September 11th, 2001, proved that. It may be but a sample of what's to come.

While the premise of Islam is to worship Allah and obey His will, the underlying motivation for the perpetual invasion of other civilizations throughout 1400 years, is total control of the masses. By instilling religious doctrine, brainwashing children and striking terror in the hearts of human beings, Islam rules with an iron fist, its leaders emboldened with the ultimate aphrodisiac: Power.

The so-called religion of peace has brought about chaos and murder in the world to a level which we have never known before, not even during the Holocaust.

Credit is due to the ingenious tactics deployed by Muslims which account for the world-wide spread of Islam. Once dominion was established in nations around the globe through murder, fear and intimidation, the next step toward expansionism and control, was to indoctrinate the children. Children of Islam all grow into adulthood where they have children of their own, and they perpetuate the indoctrination process through forthcoming generations. Muslims learned that if you take a small baby and force-feed Islam via the Quran from the age of two, they become fully programmed to deploy the will of Allah, even if it means terminating their own lives.

It's not much different than Hitler's brainwashing of Nazi youth, or the Ku Klux Klan indoctrinating little kids with hatred of Jews and Negroes. They grow up with prejudices obtained innocently at the will of fanatic adults who, like them, were propagandized in their youth.

Once two or three generations of Muslim children are fully brainwashed, they pass on that dogma to following generations, which has passed through fourteen centuries until today. Multiply that by millions and now billions living within the dark, narrow closets of Islam, and we have the world's second largest religion, and probably soon to become number one. Have no doubts, once Islam assumes dominance over any countries in Europe, as is likely in the next twenty to thirty years, converters will line up in droves outside the doors to mosques, because living under strict Islamic rule as a non-Muslim will either be illegal, or hell on earth. Peace, therefore, comes at a price.

<u>Moderate Muslims</u>

According to Dr. Ali Sina, author and former Muslim:

"The only disagreement between a moderate and terrorist Muslims is when and how the jihad against the infidels should take place. Otherwise, all the Muslims, whether moderate or extreme, believe in the same book. That book calls for waging war against the non-Muslims until they are

subdued and humiliated."

Muzammil H. Siddiqi is a Harvard-educated imam, highly regarded as a moderate among Muslim and non-Muslim circles, including the president of the United States. He stood with G.W. Bush during the post 9/11 services at the National Cathedral in 2001 to represent the Muslim faith and to condemn the attack against America. Weeks later, he was an honored guest of the president at the White House where Mr. Bush was given a copy of the Quran.

However, during a rally one year before, Siddiqi had given a speech across from that same White House where he and other Muslim leaders praised Palestinian terrorists and issued a warning to Americans to side with Palestinian Muslims against the Jews, or face Allah's punishment. Compared to notorious terrorist, Abu Musab al Zarqawi, he might be considered moderate. At least, he doesn't chop off heads from infidels.

In 2003, Siddiqi issued a fatwa, or religious decree to the Fiqh Council of North America: "... *As Muslims we should participate in the (American) system to safeguard our interests and try to bring gradual change. We must not forget that Allah's rules have to be established in all lands, and all our efforts should lead in that direction.*"

Well, that could be considered a moderate way of declaring intent to conquer. At least he didn't blow himself up in a crowded New York restaurant.

Omar M. Ahmad is another moderate Muslim leader who helped to establish the Council on American-Islamic Relations, (CAIR) a powerful lobbying group based in Washington. He also had been an honored guest at the White House, and invited by the president to join the day of mourning at the National Cathedral after 9/11.

This is what the so-called moderate Muslim said at an Islamic conference in Fremont, California in 1998:

"Islam isn't in America to be equal to any other faith but to become dominant. The Quran should be the highest authority in America and Islam the only accepted religion on earth."

Imam Siraj Wahhaj is an American black who converted to Islam and became a recognized leader in the Muslim community, particularly in Brooklyn where he does most of his preaching. Dubbed a moderate by government officials, Wahhaj holds the honor of being the first Muslim ever to give opening prayer in the U.S. Congress. He was the recipient of commendations from police for helping to drive out crime in the neighborhoods. Brooklyn authorities proclaimed a day in Wahhaj's name for his giving of "outstanding and meaningful achievements."

How can government officials be so fooled? Or perhaps, they are blind from burying their heads so deep in the sand. The same year he led the prayer in congress, 1991, he gave a speech to Muslims in Texas where he predicted that America would fall unless it accepts the Islamic agenda.

In another speech in New Jersey, Wahhaj was heard to say, *"Take my word for it, if six to eight million Muslims unite in America, the country will come to us."*

This so-called moderate Muslim hosted the blind Sheikh, Omar Abdel-Rahman at his Brooklyn mosque, the same man convicted of the first World Trade Center bombing. He even appeared in court as his character witness.

These examples represent the tip of the iceberg. While the major goal of militant Islam is to convert the world, the people who are instrumental in achieving that make no bones about deception. They know it is vital, at this point, to portray themselves as "moderate", and a non-threat, blending in with the American mainstream. But it also a sham, designed to dupe every American, from the side streets of Wichita, to the Oval Office, until Sharia law finally takes effect, and we are all in submission to Allah. Is it any wonder, then, that informed people, sadly, will trust no Muslim. What's worrisome is how grossly uninformed — or ignorant — our government really is.

In fact, there are progressive or liberal Muslims who renounce violence and do not seek conquest, but their numbers have been too few to make a difference in the trends toward violence or subversive takeover. Liberal Muslims have tended to reinterpret many aspects of their religion, particularly those who find themselves living in non-Muslim countries like the U.S. Such people describe themselves variously as progressive or reformist. These terms incorporate a broad spectrum of views which contest medievalist and traditional interpretations of Islam in many different ways.

One such Muslim, Ali Minai, a Pakistani-born professor at the University of Cincinnati, writes, "*A liberal humanist Muslim can find enough in the Islamic texts to justify a peaceful view of Islam, and this is being done with great fervor these days. A militant Muslim seeking sanction for violence, however, can also find plenty in the same sources to proclaim holy war on the world.*"

Liberal Muslims often drop traditional interpretations of the Quran which they find too conservative, preferring instead readings which are more adaptable to modern society. These Muslims reject derivation of Islamic laws from literal readings of single Quranic verses. They generally claim that a holistic view which takes into account the seventh century Arabian cultural context negates such literal interpretations. For example, some liberals may tolerate homosexuality even though conservatives forbid it.

The reliability and applicability of Hadith literature is questioned by liberals, as much of traditional Islamic law derives from it. Most liberal Muslims consequently do not believe in the authority of traditional scholars to issue a fatwa favoring instead each individual's ability to interpret Islamic sacred texts on their own.

Tolerance is another major issue. Liberal Muslims are generally open to interfaith dialogue and differences, including those among the Jewish faith. They also oppose the idea of jihad as armed struggle and tend toward ideals that are non-violent. However, in the overall scheme of things, even the liberal Muslims are aware that they will be among the chosen if and when jihad is successful and America is fully Islamicized. Thus, we must never forget that their loyalty is to Allah first. Their nation, their government and even their families, come a distant second. Whether or not they choose to interpret less strictly, they still subscribe to the same Quran, which clearly spells out Allah's decree that all the world shall one day submit to Islamic thought.

It has been said, the only difference between a radical Islamic, and a moderate, is patience.

"Oh Prophet, strive hard against the unbelievers and the hypocrites and be unyielding to them; and their abode is hell, and evil is the destination."

—From the Quran. Surah 9.73
Non-Muslims, beware.

A Violent Legacy

More people are killed by Islamists each year than in all 350 years of the Spanish Inquisition.

Islamic terrorists murder more people every day than the Ku Klux Klan has in the last 50 years.

More civilians were murdered by Muslim extremists in two hours on September 11th, 2001, than in the 36 years of sectarian conflict in Northern Ireland.

Between 2001 and 2005, outside the wars in Afghanistan and Iraq, more than 3,000 acts of terror were committed around the world by Islamofascists, resulting in the deaths of more than 6,000 innocent human beings, not to mention the thousands more that have been maimed and crippled for life. During the thirty years prior, they committed another 15,000 acts of terror, i.e. bombings, kidnappings, shootings, beheadings, and hijackings, resulting in the murder of another 30,000 people. No place on earth has been immune. Suicide bombings, alone, have occurred in over 30 countries.

While fanatics had sporadically used the tactic in years past, the suicide bomber emerged during the late 1980's as a new and ubiquitous weapon by Islamics, deployed in the midst of civilian tranquility, not the battlefield. Jihadists are dispatched by Islamics who are able to penetrate unnoticed into the innermost fabric of a society before pulling the cord to do nothing else but to murder the masses at the will of Allah. In all of history, invading armies and insurgents were limited by the quest for self-survival. But the Islamofascists came up with a tactic to develop the bombers by the thousands by brainwashing young people into believing a greater life lay ahead if they killed infidels at the beckoning of Allah.

Some tactics by terrorists are beyond horrifying, like kidnaping and killing eleven Olympic athletes at the winter games in 1972 Munich. Imagine the cold-blooded nature when they seized the Achilles Laurel cruise boat in 1985 on the Mediterranean with 400 people aboard, then unceremoniously disposed of 69 year-old Leon Klinghoffer by throwing him and his wheelchair overboard. The 2002 brutal kidnaping and taped murder in Pakistan of American journalist Daniel Pearl triggered a wave of taped beheadings of innocent workers by Islamic jihadists in Iraq and other places.

The largest Muslim nation in the world, Indonesia, is also considered among the more moderate. But they have also been marked with a history of violence and intolerance of any other religion. In October of 2005, three Christian girls attending a private high school were ambushed and beheaded by Islamic fanatics while walking home from their class. They were killed for no other reason than their faith. In the ten years prior, some 12,000 Christians were likewise beheaded, knifed, bombed or gunned down in an ongoing effort to rid the country of it's Christians which make up only eight percent of the population. During it thirty-year struggle for independence, the tiny Christian enclave of West Timor lost over 300,000 souls.

The beat goes on. The bombing in London in 2005. The bombings in Spain of 2004. The Muslim riots in France of 2005. The violent uprisings around the world in February of 2006 following the infamous Denmark cartoons of Muhammad. The entire world is holding their breath in wait for the next slaughter by militant Islamics who justify murder in the name of Allah. People everywhere avoid flying, cruising and commuting lest they become victim to the next whim of violence by Islamic jihadists. We all know they are out there, plotting to kill. It's not a matter of if, it's a matter of when, where and how. And for certain, the United States — considered by Islamic jihadists to be the great Satan and the next *dar al-harb* (Land of War) — would be the ultimate prize.

A state of fear has been instilled into innocent people around the world, and it is the product of none other than delegates of a peaceful religion.

<u>The Quran</u>

No Muslim can claim devotion to their religion without accepting, unconditionally, the totality of their holy book. No different than Christians who revere the bible as gospel, particularly the New Testament, Muslims adhere to the rules and verses contained in the Quran. That is required of all Muslims, whether they be deemed radical or moderate. The Quran is the focal point of all Muslims, regarded by most as the word of God, written on golden tablets in Paradise.

With that in mind, and having heard the rhetoric that Islam is a peaceful religion, and that the Quran is Allah's book of goodness, tolerance, guidance and love, I visited several on-line web sites and reviewed a number of *surah* (chapters) and verses (*aya*), many of which deal with conditions of behavior, treatment of women, mandates about praising and worshiping Allah and so forth. But I wondered also, if there were any references to violence, intolerance or hate, so I entered one single word in the "search" box: *Unbelievers.* After all, we know the militant Muslims obsess on infidels.

Out of 114 *surah* and more than six thousand *aya*, I found at least 120 references to "unbelievers" (non-Muslims), most of which were rather unfriendly. (Compare to 83 for "love") In fact, the Quran appears quite hostile to those of us who believe differently.

Here are some examples of how Islam's holy book views people who do not share the same religious convictions.

"Evil is that for which they have sold their souls...that they should deny what Allah has revealed , out of envy that Allah should send down of His grace on whomever of His servants He pleases; so they have made themselves deserving of wrath upon wrath and there is a disgraceful punishment for the unbelievers."
Surah — 2:89

"Whoever is the enemy of Allah and His angels and His apostles and Jibreel and Meekaeel, so surely Allah is the enemy of the unbelievers."
Surah — 2:98

"And kill them wherever you find them, and drive them out from whence they drove you out, and persecution is severer than slaughter, and do not fight with them at the Sacred Mosque until they fight with you in it, but if they do fight you, then slay them; such is the recompense of the unbelievers."
Surah — 2:191

They have invaded our military, colleges, prison systems, law enforcement agencies, and worst of all, our national government. And it is all within the full view and knowledge of America, under protection of the very constitution they wish to destroy.

Author Abdullah Al-Araby, a former mid-east Muslim, tells us that our enemy has deployed five weapons for the Islamization of America: Lying, Sex, Race, Money and Terror. They use these weapons without reservation if it is to further their goal.

Lying and deception.

Many Muslim supporters, or so-called "moderate" Muslims present a polished version of Islam to Americans in order to create the perception that they are a peaceful and generous people, with only a tiny rogue faction causing problems. In truth, Islam sanctions deception and lies in order to further the long range plan to serve Allah and for world conquest. This is why we cannot trust any nation that is one hundred percent Muslim — such as Saudi Arabia — that purports to be our friend, who impress us all by dispatching articulate and educated ambassadors for interviews on CNN, who tell us they want to live in peace with the west. That may be true for the moment, but we must realize they are fully focused on the long term objectives.

We cannot lose sight of the fact that the Saudis harbor terrorists, funnel money to terrorists, reward "martyr" families for acts of terror and house one of the most extreme and oppressive forms of Islam in the world — Wahhabism, which is the government religion of Saudi Arabia. That is why informed Americans cringe at the sight of a crowned Saudi prince and the President of the United States holding hands, as they did in Texas in April of 2005. One can only surmise that our president is ill-informed, ignorant or just plain stupid. Either that or the Bush dynasty has irreversible and vested interests with the Saudi Kingdom, who is seemingly immune from government scrutiny here in the U.S. As we'll see, the Bush clan has been chummy with the Saudis for more than thirty years.

How can we trust our government if it trusts those who cannot be trusted?

Muslims will tell you that the Quran forbids lying and therefore all truths be told. But we know from recorded history how many times an Islamic nation has said one thing then done another. That is how they have won many conflicts and conquered nations over the centuries.

Israel is the greatest example of a nation who has fallen victim to incessant broken agreements and cease-fires by Muslims, only to have their citizens die violently over and over again in suicide bombings and unprovoked mortar attacks. While the Quran forbids lying, it also provides for exceptions when it is necessary to serve the will of Allah.

"Allah does not call you to account for what is vain in your oaths, but He will call you to account for what your hearts have earned, and Allah is Forgiving, Forbearing."
— Surah 2.225

According to Islam, war is deception and necessarily justifies the forbidden. Those kind of rules basically give license to militant Muslims to do as they wish, when and how they wish, so long as they rationalize it as an act of war.

In the Hadith, one of Muhammad's daughters, Umm Kalthoum testified that her father condoned lying in three situations:
* For reconciliation among people
* Among spouses to keep the peace
* In war (i.e. today's jihad)

Many Muslim clerics and other leaders cannot be trusted no matter what they say, because the higher authority of Muhammad, and the Quran, take precedence over all. Muslims will often quote selective verses from the Quran to point out the misconceptions of Islam, and to convince us all that it is a religion based on truth.

Al Araby interestingly points out:

"An example of Islamic deception is that Muslim activists always quote passages of the Quran from the early part of Muhammad's ministry while living in Mecca. These texts are peaceful and exemplify tolerance toward those who are not followers of Islam. They are fully aware that these passages were abrogated by later passages after he migrated to Medina." (After Muhammad took up the sword in 622 A.D.)

There are Islamic clerics who have stated that the attacks on 9/11 were committed by the U.S. government, and blamed on Islamics. Some have lamented the 9/11 attacks to government officials then cheered them during private sermons inside the mosque. The new president of Iran, strict Islamic Mahmoud Ahmadinejad, has made several public statements saying that the Holocaust never happened. In eighth grade Palestinian classrooms, children are presented with maps of the world, absent the existence of Israel.

"*The Spirit Of Islam,*" was written by the Muslim scholar, Afif A. Tabbarah, to promote his religion. On page 247, Tabbarah wrote:

"*Lying is not always bad, to be sure; there are times when telling a lie is more profitable and better for the general welfare, and for the settlement of conciliation among people, than telling the truth. To this effect, the Prophet says: 'He is not a false person who (through lies) settles conciliation among people, supports good or says what is good.'*"

Sex.

In most Muslim societies, women within the Muslim grasp are, by law, second-rate citizens. In some places, they are considered property on a par with owning a camel. They use, feed, beat and discard them when no longer obedient or useful. Saudi women are virtual slaves to men, whether they be fathers, brothers or husbands. They may not drive a car, they may not make eye contact with other men, they may not travel or attend school without permission from their master. They are subject to brutal methods of punishment for deeds that are not even considered an offense in the United States.

In his book, "*Sexuality and Eroticism Among Males in Moslem Societies*", Maarten Schild states that Islamic law considers female same-sex behavior as "sex outside marriage and therefore as adultery" for which the traditional punishment is death by stoning for married people, and 100 lashes for unmarried people.

"Men are the maintainers of women because Allah has made some of them to excel others and because they spend out of their property; the good women are therefore obedient, guarding the unseen as Allah has guarded; and (as to) those on whose part you fear desertion, admonish them, and leave them alone in the sleeping-places and beat them; then if they obey you, do not seek a way against them; surely Allah is High, Great."

—Surah 4.34

Women who marry Muslims are supposed to be virgins before marriage. In fact, if it learned that a woman has had sex before marriage then, quite often, she is killed by a male member of her family. Thousands of such crimes of "honor" occur in many Muslim countries today, as well as some non-Muslim countries, and the males are rarely punished. In fact, the perpetrators are looked upon as heroes for restoring their families "honor".

Even in marriage, sexual inequality is pervasive. According to Islamic tradition men must always be dominant, even in bed. A female is not allowed to be on top when making love to a man. Any sexual position where the female is on top is considered haram or sinful.

But Islam does not unveil this constricting form of male/female relationships in America or Europe. That's because one of the tactics being used for converting the west is to recruit more Muslims among the American people.

As part of the strategy, Arab-based Muslim men have effectively spread Islam in America by marrying non-Muslim women. These men aren't doing this because they are falling in love, any more than they are falling in love with America. They are doing it as a duty to Allah to further the plan of conquest. Not only that, it provides mid-east Muslims residency status to remain legally in the United States from where they can continue clandestine anti-American activities. They procreate prolifically, bearing five to ten children per family, adding even more to the burgeoning Muslim population. Mixed breed children are of great value. With predominantly Caucasian or Negroid features, they will be less conspicuous amid the general population, thus highly valued as soldiers of jihad.

Mid-east men can be quite romantic and attractive to American women, especially those who have difficulty attracting a relationship. They may be told that they can retain their Christian faith, that it is compatible with Islam. In long run, that is a lie. When the honeymoon period is over, Muslim husbands will pressure women to convert and demand that their children be raised as Muslims. If the woman wants to leave the marriage or leave the faith, she cannot take the children with her, because they belong to the father, under Islamic law. Plus, she is not entitled to any support. If the woman does leave, the husband will have performed his duty by bringing several new Muslims into the world.

It is estimated that 10,000 to 15,000 American women are marrying Muslim men every year. Multiply this with the numbers of offspring procreating in twenty more years just as prolifically. This has been going on in Europe, where Muslim populations are rapidly growing into more influential numbers. And it does not include the millions of mid-east Muslims who are procreating among themselves. Add this to the rapid rate of conversions and immigration in the U.S., one only has to do the math to see where this is going.

Every so often, my wife and I will visit a shopping mall and see an American woman working in a gift shop wearing a hijab. For the most part, these women are less than physically attractive leading us to believe that many are thrilled just to be cared for and taken as a wife. We know the store brings in profits that are not only used to support her family, a percentage of the money is sent overseas in support of the international Islamic movement. And more than likely, this unfortunate woman has been duped, her future life destined toward misery and slavery.

Journalist Laura Mansfield tells of a learning session she attended at a mosque in a small southern town. She posed as a woman interested in a possible conversion. Dressed in casual western garb, she arrived an hour earlier than the scheduled session to find that men, and only men, were present. She asked the imam there if she could just sit and wait in the back of the room for the hour while she read. He hesitated, then agreed. Then she overheard him telling the others not to worry, she was an American who did not speak Arabic.

But she did. What she overheard from that point on was chilling, as men openly talked about justifying civil disobedience in America, spreading words of hate and defiance to everyone in the congregation. The imam closed the session by reminding everyone it was their duty as Muslims to continue in the path of jihad, by using either subtle and simple methods, or by terrorism, or the support of terrorism. This — in small town America. Imagine

Detroit? Chicago?

The problem, is that Americans are made to believe that this kind of teaching is among the minority of Muslims when, in fact, it is the majority.

When the groups of women arrived an hour later, Mansfield noticed that the tone was completely different when related in English. The head female speaker focused on the similarities between Christianity and Islam, emphasizing how peaceful and loving and misunderstood the religion really was. In the previous session, the men had quoted over and over again many surah from the Quran calling for violent jihad, while the women's session focused on the "gentler" side of Islam. What they omitted, was the full story, as quoted in the Quran, such as:

> *"Your wives are a tilth (tilled soil) for you, so go into your tilth when you like, and do good beforehand for yourselves, and be careful (of your duty) to Allah, and know that you will meet Him, and give good news to the believers."*
>
> —Surah 2.223

The same imam who preached to the men to continue in the path of jihad had done a complete 180-degree turn for the women, stressing only the surahs that promote "brotherhood" between Muslims, Christians and Jews. The differences between the sessions were striking. The second session was obviously tempered to stimulate recruitment.

The public image of Islam is carefully honed to fool people and present a visage of peace and tranquility while private interaction behind closed doors is another story. It's reminiscent of the Mafia, whose men are notorious for keeping their women detached from the murderous side of their lives while maintaining a dual role as devoted fathers and husbands. Their women were either ignorant, uninformed or they turned a blind eye, gladly accepting the benefits afforded them and ignoring the evil. It's not much different with the Muslims.

Based on a true story, the movie, *Not Without My Daughter,* released in 1991 and starring Sally Field, is a startling example of how American women are lured into the Islamic trap, only to find out later they are really nothing more than a slave.

In this docudrama, a mid-'80s Michigan housewife, Betty Mahmoody, has a five-year-old daughter while married to an Iranian doctor. Her life turns upside down when a two-week vacation to Tehran with her husband turns into virtual imprisonment for her and her child. Reluctant at first, she agrees to go because of her husband's problems with racism in America and his yearning for contact with his family.

Islamic fundamentalism and strange customs of Iran bewilder and frighten Betty and her daughter, Mahtob, but nothing prepares her for his surprise announcement that they will not return to the U.S. and will remain in Tehran indefinitely. Despite beatings (which is permitted when a wife is non-obedient) and more pervasive psychological control from her husband and his relatives, Betty makes it to the Swiss embassy (there is no American ambassador). There, she learns that as the wife of an Iranian, she is now considered a citizen and that she has absolutely no parental rights over Mahtob (the daughter) in the country. Betty endures several years as a virtual prisoner, eventually escaping with her daughter with the help of Westernized Iranian friends.

Race.

Militant Muslims use the race card by creating division among Americans on our own soil. The history of slavery is often exploited and belabored in order to instill more hatred and animosity toward white America. Once the American black is primed, Islam moves in by demonstrating how much they are loved and protected by Allah. What they don't tell African-Americans, is that black slavery existed long before whites migrated to the new world. The biggest slave traders and owners in the world were the Arabs of many centuries before, the prophet Muhammed being one of them, owning many slaves of his own. Saudi Arabia did not abolish slavery until 1962.

African-Americans are actively recruited in the military, prisons and juvenile detention facilities where a large reservoir of negative attitudes toward America already exist. Disenfranchised and bitter at the world, many blacks in prison are prime targets for conversion. It is estimated that 200,000 inmates in the U.S. have converted to the Islamic faith, not only because they accept belief in Allah and the Quran, they are promised — and provided — a substantial degree of protection from other hostile inmates in the system. That makes for a great sales pitch, especially for those doomed to many years. For those close to parole, it provides support and sanctuary to those hostile to the American way, which plays right into the hands of militant Islam.

Today, nearly three of the seven million Muslims in America, are African-American. Many have become clerics who preach jihad, and recruit new Muslims into the cause.

<u>Money.</u>

Besides acts of terror, this is the most powerful tool of militant Islam for the ultimate Islamization of America. Until the second half of the 20th century, Arab lands where Islam prevailed were not considered a threat, because they were basically isolated from the rest of the world. Then came the nascent dependency on petroleum which comes from crude oil harvested in the mid-east. The enormous wealth in Saudi Arabia has catapulted them into one of the greatest financial powers in the world. With such wealth, comes influence. They hold Europe, Asia, Africa, South and North America in an economic stranglehold. While options to change this pattern have not been actively pursued by our government, we all continue to suck off the mid-east teat, then complain about world terrorism which has been financed, directly or indirectly by our own dollars.

Mosques and Islamic learning centers are sprouting up by the thousands all over Europe and the United States, tripling in the last twenty years. The Barnabas Fund reported that more than half of the 1,300 mosques in America have been built with Saudi money, while eighty percent continue to be under control of Saudi Wahhabists. In essence, Saudis, and other similar governments, are using their enormous wealth to export their ideology to America with the same long range goals in mind:

Islamic expansionism.

The Saudis are also funding the establishment of secular colleges and universities. Millions of dollars have been funneled to non-Muslim students as grants to study at Islamic schools. The obvious aim is to evangelize and convert as many young people as possible.

Al Araby writes:

"A 34-page report submitted to the United Nations in December 2002 concluded that despite a crackdown on terrorism financing after September 11th, Saudi Arabia must still dismantle a system that has permitted hundreds of millions of dollars to flow to Islamic extremists through businesses and charities."

French investigator Jean-Charles Brisard, co-author of *Forbidden Truth*, tells us that al Qaeda received between $300 and $500 million over a ten year period 1992 - 2002, from wealthy businessmen and bankers whose fortunes represent about twenty percent of the Saudi GNP, through a web of charities and companies acting as fronts.

As a supplement to oil-based funding, al Qaeda has acquired much needed weapons and supplies via the vast resource available through international drug smuggling, namely heroin. Afghanistan, which is seeing a resurgence of the Taliban, produces 80 percent of the world's poppy fields, which not only helps to support the rural farmer in that country, it feeds the kitty for international terror.

Of course, much of the world's terrorism has been financed through donations small and large, made by Muslims around the world, particularly from the

Unites States. Hundreds of mosques and learning centers serve as filtering centers for donations under the cloak of religious exemption, in which the real destination for their charity goes toward funding jihad.

Terror.

"Terrorism" is a term so often used in today's vernacular that we tend to forget it's true meaning. Terrorism is not just the use of violence, it is the deliberate killing of innocent human beings — men, women and children — usually en masse, and usually not directed toward a military enemy. It's pure murder. Nothing else.

The world, including the United States, has suffered thousands of murderous acts inflicted against innocent people for the last forty years, 99 percent by militant Islamics claiming to represent the will of Allah.

Terrorists not only kill, they maim, they leave innocent people blind, deaf, armless and legless, not to mention the psychological trauma imposed for life. The sheer acts of murder intimidate those left alive into compliance with their wishes. Consider Spain, the Philippines and other nations that have backed out of Iraq after carefully planned attacks and kidnapings of their people, some of which resulted in death. Look at Germany that capitulated to terror and released the three remaining terrorist killers of the Israeli Olympic athletes in 1972. Italy was so intimidated by Islamic threats, that they released the killer who masterminded the hijacking of the passenger ship Achille Lauro in 1985. Until September 11th, America had been lulled into thinking that real terror happens elsewhere, not inside our own borders. Now we know different, but as time passes and we become complacent, we may be inviting more of the same, and worse.

Terror works. It enables a minority to dominate a majority. It has been the catalyst that formed the Islamic world 1400 years ago. It is the catalyst that is changing the world in 2006.

The so-called war on terror is being waged on two distinct fronts, operating independently but woven by a common goal. One is militarily, in theaters of operation in Iraq and Afghanistan. The other, and far more dangerous, is the massive infiltration of militant Islam into our nation with the deliberate intention of Islamizing our cities, towns, government institutions and our people. Freedoms, as we know them today, will become obsolete. The takeover is inevitable unless we open our eyes and see the reality, not the smokescreen, not the fantasy, not the politically correct religion of peace, but the cold hard truth.

Our government tells us that they have crushed the Taliban in Afghanistan and have set up a democracy in Iraq. While that is arguable, they are not telling us is that the proliferation of militant Islam is actually succeeding around the globe, and that the money and leadership that supports that effort is thriving. All that we hear from Dick Cheney, Donald Rumsfeld, Condoleeza Rice and G.W. Bush about "winning" is political rhetoric directed toward naive Americans.

The future capture and/or killing of Osama Bin Laden, or his top henchmen, would suggest that we will have dealt a serious blow to the brain trust of militant Islam. Not true. Without a doubt, Osama bin Laden has arranged for a succession of command so that the momentum will not be interrupted no matter who takes the helm. Remember, the real leader is Allah.

We will never see Allah sitting down on the deck of a warship signing a formal surrender. There is no such thing as winning this war, because no one can truly define "winning." The best we can do is stem the tide of Islamic proliferation and contain the jihad to impotent status.

Dr. Shorrosh's Prognostication:

Dr. Anis Shorrosh is a Palestinian Arab Christian American and a member of Oxford Society of Scholars. A recognized authority on mid-east Islamic studies, he has traveled in 76 countries as an author, lecturer and producer of TV documentaries. He is author of several best sellers, including *"Islam Revealed"* and *"Islam: A Threat or a Challenge."* He has written his own grim prognostications on Islam's strategy for conquering America in the next twenty years.

* Terminate America's freedom of speech by replacing it with hate crime bills statewide and nationwide.

* Wage a war of words using black leaders like Louis Farrakhan, Rev. Jesse Jackson and other visible religious personalities to promote Islam as the original African-American's religion while Christianity is for the whites!

* Engage the American public in dialogues, discussions, debates in colleges, universities, public libraries, radio, TV, churches and mosques on the virtues of Islam.

* Nominate Muslim sympathizers to political office for favorable legislation to Islam and support potential sympathizers by block voting.

* Take control of as much of Hollywood, the press, TV, radio and the internet by buying the corporations or a controlling stock.

* Yield to the fear of imminent shut-off of the lifeblood of America - the black gold.

* Yell, "foul, out-of-context, personal interpretation, hate crime, Zionist, un-American, inaccurate interpretation of the Quran" anytime Islam is criticized or the Quran is analyzed in the public arena.

* Encourage Muslims to penetrate the White House, specifically with Islamists who can articulate a marvelous and peaceful picture of Islam. Acquire government positions, get membership in local school boards. Train Muslims as medical doctors to dominate the medical field, research and pharmaceutical companies. Take over the computer industry.

* Accelerate Islamic demographic growth via massive immigration, no birth control whatsoever

* Muslim men must marry American women and Islamize them. Then divorce them and remarry every five years - since one cannot have the Muslim legal permission to marry four at one time.

* Convert angry, alienated black inmates and turn them into militants (so far 2,000 released inmates have joined al Qaeda world-wide).

* Reading, writing, arithmetic and research through the American educational system, mosques and student centers should be sprinkled with dislike of Jews, evangelical Christians and democracy.

* Provide very sizeable monetary Muslim grants

to colleges and universities in America to establish "Centers for Islamic studies" with Muslim directors to promote Islam in higher education institutions.

* Appeal to the historically compassionate and sensitive Americans for sympathy and tolerance towards the Muslims in America who are portrayed as mainly immigrants from oppressed countries.

* Nullify America's sense of security by manipulating the intelligence community with misinformation. Periodically terrorize Americans of impending attacks on bridges, tunnels, water supplies, airports, apartment buildings and malls.

* Form riots and demonstrations in the prison system demanding Islamic Sharia as the way of life, not America's justice system.

* Open numerous charities throughout the U.S. but use the funds to support Islamic terrorism with American dollars.

* Raise interest in Islam on America's campuses by insisting that freshman take at least one course on Islam.

* Send intimidating messages and messengers to the outspoken individuals who are critical of Islam and seek to eliminate them by hook or crook.

* Applaud Muslims as loyal citizens of the U.S. by spotlighting their voting record as the highest percentage of all minority and ethic groups in America.

Like Abdullah Al-Araby, Dr. Shorrosh is among thousands of scholars and experts who are sounding the alarm. Are we listening?

The Trojan Horse

I was but a young homicide detective when a wise lieutenant named Chuck Harbolt said to me, "Look for the simple answer. If it stares you in the face, don't ignore it." Well, this is staring us in the face, and we are ignoring it.

I believe Osama has outsmarted us, more than we realize.

While America fights terrorism around the globe, we may have lost sight of the larger picture. If so, the land of the free should change its focus very soon, or it may be doomed. Al Qaeda's ploy may have been to see us extend our military forces and our billions of war dollars overseas while radical Islam surreptitiously roots into the fabric of American society. We've been caught looking the other way. And while the president holds one hand with the Saudi sheiks, they're stabbing him in the back with the other hand.

The attacks of 9/11/01 was a wake-up call that jihad is not some insignificant entity of crazy terrorists that we have to deal with now and then. It's an enemy powerful and determined enough to bring America to its knees. It would not only be naive, but pure stupid to assume it's all the product of al Qaeda.

I've heard sympathizers argue that there have been other terrorists who are non-Muslim Americans, that people like myself are discriminating. Sure, Timothy McVeigh blew up a building in Oklahoma City, and Eric Rudolph killed some folks with his bombs. There's two. They were isolated whackos with a personal ax to grind. So was Jack the Ripper. But they did not represent a viable and dangerous form of government. They are like a couple of pole beans in a corn field, insignificant compared to the international conspiracy called jihad, funded by billions of oil dollars, systematically deploying an unlimited army of suicide killers around the globe for the expressed purpose of reversing our way of life.

I see a much bigger picture than the 9/11 attacks, or the wars in Afghanistan and Iraq. Osama cast the bait, and the USA chomped like a speckled trout, sending our military overseas to fight conventional wars, chase after foreign terrorists and divert our attention from the more clandestine and serious threat which lies inside our very borders. While the administration targets far-away lands, weapons of mass destruction are being cultivated right here...in a manner not dreamed of.

Terrorism in the U.S. is an easy matter. Timothy McVeigh had no problem killing 168 Americans in one day. So why have there been no terrorist attacks since September 11th, 2001? I believe it has nothing to do with the administration's success in tightening security, which has not improved very much. It's part of their strategy. Militant Islam is very patient. Al Qaeda wants us running in the wrong direction while they pursue their deadly agenda under our very noses. I believe, the most ominous threat festers within as the Trojan horse of the 21st century:

The mosque.

In 2004, columnist Cal Thomas warned us that, "a training ground of hate currently exists on American soil." Innocent little children born to Islamic radicals are being raised like farm animals by the thousands, brainwashed twenty-four hours a day inside Muslim homes and mosques throughout

America to hate Jews, hate Americans and all infidels in the name of Allah, and to look forward to the day of glory when they will ascend to the great God by killing them all. When the attacks begin, we may see them as teenage insurgents, but in truth, they will be products of a carefully calculated ten or fifteen-year plan that cultivated and hypnotized them as human weapons of mass destruction. Imagine, for one moment, fifty or five hundred suicide bombers inside America, at one time. By the time it starts, it may be too late.

The irony is that these plots are being carried out under the protection of the very constitution they wish to destroy. The freedoms of assembly, freedoms of speech and— most importantly — freedom of religion, are the protections which these fanatics are using to eradicate America. One wonders what Mr. Jefferson or Mr. Madison would think if they knew the Bill of Rights was being exploited by foreigners as a tool to destroy America — with our permission. And it is all being plotted, financed and controlled by our two-faced friends in the mid-east: Saudi Arabia.

"The Islamic invasion of America is an agenda of Islamists with visible methods to take over America by the year 2020! Will Americans continue to sleep through this invasion as they did when we were attacked on 9/11?"

—Dr. Anis Shorrosh, author and mid-east expert

CHAPTER THREE

THE SAUDI CONNECTION

Within three days after the 9/11 hijackings, while America's airways were still closed to all commercial airline traffic and the president was declaring a war against terrorism, 142 influential Saudis visiting the U.S. were allowed a hasty departure by the White House to fly out of the country and back to their homeland. Two of them were relatives of Osama bin Laden. This was an elaborate but hurried evacuation in which the Saudis were picked up from ten different U.S. cities before shuttled out of the country, courtesy of the U.S. government.

FBI officials claimed that some were dutifully interviewed before the departure, including the bin Laden relatives. However, former agent, Dale Watson, who once headed counter-terrorism at the FBI, said, "They were not subject to serious interviews or interrogations."

As a homicide investigator, I interviewed thousands of people, assembling background information, presenting cold-hard evidence to a subject then putting the squeeze on with tough questions. It's important to follow-up and investigate the validity of a person's denial, and re-interview if necessary, offering a subject opportunities to take a polygraph if warranted.

I can just see the nature of these "interviews."

"Mr. Sheik, excuse me sir, did you have anything to do with the 9/11 massacre?" Mr. Sheik answers "no", and that ends that. No further inquiry needed, even though our nation is under attack, 3,000 innocent people have just been murdered and a possible link to the perpetrators is within our immediate grasp. Instead, politics — as usual — took priority. So much for an aggressive fight against terrorism. So much for playing hard ball.

Intelligence and media sources knew, almost immediately, the names and personal data concerning Osama bin Laden and the nineteen hijackers. It would be plausible, then, that all foreign visitors of Arab/Islamic orientation — especially Saudis — should have been investigated thoroughly before being allowed to disappear back into the mid-east netherland. As a career cop, I can assure anyone that it would be impossible to resolve any suspicions or links of the Saudis to 9/11 in such a complicated matter in one brief interview. The FBI certainly knew that. But, they apparently had to answer to a higher power.

The Bush administration dismissed the incident saying, basically, that they were afraid the Saudis would suffer retribution by Americans if allowed to remain. One wonders, then, why we didn't escort another five million Arab Islamics out at the same time? That is, if they feared an American revolt against Muslims.

At least one senator, Charles Schumer, of New

York, had serious issues with the decision. *"This is just another example of our country coddling the Saudis and giving them special privileges that others would never get,"* he said. *"It's almost as if we didn't want to find out what links existed."*

Coddling, indeed.

Our government often speaks out against countries who have a horrid history of human rights violations, like China, North Korea, Iraq, Syria, Cuba and so forth. But what of Saudi Arabia, where women are not permitted to drive automobiles, nor perform any activity outside the home without the expressed permission of a male superior. Where laws forbid any other form of religion, and the mere possession of a Christian bible in public is considered a crime punishable by prison time and public flogging. In 2002, three Saudi men were publicly beheaded for homosexual conduct in violation of Islamic law.

Saudi Arabia practices the Wahhabi form of Islam, which is slightly less radical than the Taliban. There is only one God, one religion, and anyone who fails to believe is an infidel who must be dealt with according to God's law as spelled out in the Quran. Today, thanks to billions in petro dollars, Wahhabism is the most dominant of all Muslim sects and is spreading throughout the U.S.

As long as we suck their oil, our government representatives don't care if they are fascists, communists or Nazis. In fact, they are worse. The Nazis were not ambiguous. We knew their intent and motives from day one. We could see them, we knew their weapons and their boundaries. This is different. The Wahhabists are a deceitful and tenacious enemy who will do anything to perpetuate the Islamization of America, even if it takes another hundred years.

That's the will of Allah. We must never lose sight of that.

Muslim clerics all over the world, including many inside America, have announced their intent to convert the United States into an Islamic state. They will do it under the cloak of religious freedom, with the full love and embrace of our politically correct government until, one day, we'll look back and scratch our heads, saying, "Why didn't we see it coming?"

The Saudi Kingdom has invested over $700 billion in companies around the world, 60 percent of it in the United States. That kind of money buys a lot influence.

The foothold has taken place inside the mosque. What better launching pad for terror and influence, than one that is wholly protected as a religious site under the constitution. It's like giving the Nazis an exempt military intelligence station inside Washington D.C. in 1942, only multiply it by a thousand. In truth, mosques are serving as grandma's nightgown for the wolf in disguise who is preparing to devour Little Red Riding Hood.

Mosques and Islamic learning centers are sprouting up all over the U.S., even in places where there are no Muslims, or very few. In the last twenty years, the numbers of mosques have quadrupled to nearly 1,300 across America, which doesn't include another 500 sites designated as "learning centers." Eighty percent are financed and controlled by Saudi Arabia. In another ten years, that number will likely double.

Same with our neighbors. In Cornwall, Ontario, I saw an old hospital that had recently been converted into an Islamic Learning Center, where —

when purchased — a handful of Muslims were living in that small town. That's like building a giant synagogue in the bible belt town of Bryson City, North Carolina, where a handful of Jews reside. The proliferation of Islamic properties is going on in every major and minor city in America. Money is no problem, because American and European dollars are coming back in our own face through financial donations, the illicit drug trade and the oil loop in Saudi Arabia.

King Fahd of Saudi pledged as much as $8 million to build a new mosque at the site of the Masjid Bilal Islamic Center, the large black mosque in South Central Los Angeles. Bilal is just one of many black mosques funded by the Saudis. Most of them, including Bilal, are associated with Imam W. Deen Mohammed, head of the Chicago-based Muslim American Society, or MAS, which has been credited with helping convert more than a million U.S. blacks to Islam.

A spokesman for the group said "hundreds of American mosques are associated with MAS," explaining that each major city has "one main mosque and two or three smaller centers." The Chicago area, for example, has a MAS mosque and three related centers, he says.

In many — not all — of these so-called religious institutions, masses of children are being spoon fed hate propaganda. They also serve as a recruiting station, training ground and spiritual counseling center for terrorists. Many mosques from L.A. to Chicago to New York and Washington D.C., have been identified by law enforcement as depositories for huge sums of money listed as charity but ultimately laundered to serve the cause of jihad.

Books written by Paul Sperry and Harvey Kushner, and others, specifically identify dozens of mosques that are serving the cause of jihad. Among them:

* The Dar al-Hijrah mosque, in Falls Church, Virginia is one of the nation's largest fund raisers for the terrorist group, Hamas. Some of the 9/11 hijackers were known to receive counseling and comfort there. Author Paul Sperry describes it as a virtual "...magnet for militant Islamics. Over the years it has attracted an alarming number of terrorist supporters, terrorist facilitators, fund raisers, co-conspirators, and actual terrorists."

The huge mosque, complete with minaret and opened in 1991 at a cost of six-million dollars, was built with great consternation by residents of this old established neighborhood. What once was a charming ambience, is now a hotbed of traffic congestion where Muslims park on sidewalks, driveways, lawns, and in the middle of streets leaving trash as they go. Complaints to local officials have fallen on deaf ears.

The founder and president of this mosque, Samir Salah, has been tied to groups suspected of aiding al-Qaeda. He helped establish Bank al-Taqwa which the U.S. government has banned as a funnel agency for al-Qaeda and Hamas funding. Abdurahman Alamoudi, who founded the American Muslim Council was an influential member of the mosque and a political activist in Washington. He is now in prison for plotting acts of terror.

* Masjed As-Saber, a Sunni mosque in a suburb of Portland, Oregon where the iman, Sheik Mohamaed Abdirahman Kariye, was arrested by federal authorities as he attempted to leave the

country in 2002. FBI documents alleged that Kariiye collected thousands of dollars from mosque members to fund the efforts of the "Portland Six" to join the Taliban.

*The Al-Farooq Mosque in Brooklyn, New York was once led by blind imam, Sheik Omar Abdel-Rahman, best known for his complicity in the 1993 bombing of the World Trade Center, for which he was convicted. He had openly called for jihad against the enemies of Islam, namely the Unites States. He also visited other mosques where he called for the violent overthrow of any regime that supported Israel or the U.S.

Several other of it's imams have been known to preach hate and violence toward America, including Fawaz Abu Damra. In the 1990's, he orated, *"Direct all rifles at the first and last enemy of the Islamic nation, and this is the sons of monkeys and pigs, the Jews."* Damra later became the head of the Islamic Center of Greater Cleveland.

* Located on the first floor of an office building in Falls Church, Virginia, the Dar Al-Arqam Islamic Center has been a hotbed of anti-American activity and propaganda. Shortly after 9/11 occurred, imam Ali al-Timimi was overheard telling a group of Muslim men that America is "the greatest enemy of Muslims." After he was indicted on charges that he aided and abetted terrorists, investigators found photos of the FBI headquarters building on the computer of one of his underlings, along with a document containing instructions on how to make bombs and chemical weapons.

* The Islamic Center of San Diego, a Wahhabi mosque, is known to have provided aid and comfort to two of the 9/11 hijackers.

*   Masjid al-Hijrah is a hard-line Wahhabi mosque in Ft. Lauderdale which is known for imams that have counseled al Qaeda terrorists, and receive the lion's share of their money direct from the Saudi embassy.

*   The mosque in Lackawanna, New York, on the coast of Lake Erie, uses an abandoned Ukrainian Church. It also hosted an al Qaeda sleeper cell where six men were arrested by the FBI in 2001 for attending al Qaeda training camps in Afghanistan.

*   Then there is the famous mosque in Hamtramck, Michigan, where mainstream America is experiencing it's first public infiltration of Islam. In 2003, the city council of Hamtramck (near Detroit) buckled under to Muslim pressure and approved an Islamic call to prayer within city limits, five times a day starting at 6 a.m., over loud speakers for all to hear, and in Arabic. Local residents are outraged. Where next? Philadelphia? Miami? Green Bay? Asheville?

These are but a sampling. It would take a massive study to expose them all.

Protected by religious freedom, they have rooted in like cancer quietly eating away at our nation. Compare the state of affairs to twenty years ago, and witness their progress, then imagine the next forty years. Sixty. One hundred.

In 2002, Saudi Cleric, Shaikh Saad al-Buraik hosted a 24 hour telethon in Riyadh where $109 million was raised for Palestinian fighters and families of "martyrs." On tape, al-Buraik called for Jewish women to be enslaved, *"Muslim Brothers in Palestine, do not have any mercy nor compassion for the Jews, their blood, their money, their flesh. Their women are yours to take, legitimately. God* *made them yours. Enslave their women. Why don't you wage jihad? Why don't you pillage them?"*Then he said, *"I am against America until this life ends, until the Day of Judgement. She is the root of all evils and wickedness on earth."*

Al-Buraik is now the host of his own television show, Religion And Life, shown on a government-owned television channel.

CHAPTER FOUR

PRISONS:
FIELD OF RECRUITMENT

The recruitment of new and recusant Americans is of prime interest to the cause of Islamic expansionism. State and federal prisons have become a prime target of Wahhabists for luring converts to Islam, more so even than hard line mosques. And our tax-supported government leaders are overseeing the entire fiasco.

The National Islamic Prison Foundation claims they convert 135,000 prison inmates a year to Islam, nearly 95 percent among African American inmates. Prison officials believe that's inflated and put the number at 30,000 to 40,000, still an imposing influence. At least 300,000, or 15 percent of the 2.1 million inmates in today's system claim to be Muslim. It is a substantial number in growth, as Islam recruits convicted criminals who are graduating from our nations prisons. We are seeing many violent offenders enter into a violence-associated faith.

With their release back into society as Muslims, and after years of confinement in a criminal justice system they see as unfair to their race, they offer the perfect profile for Islam to create an abetter to terrorism.

Three such converts have gained notoriety since their release from prison:

* Richard Reid, the convicted "Shoe Bomber," was converted to Islam in a British prison by a radical imam, Abdul Ghani Qureshi, at the suggestion of his father, a Jamaican-born career criminal and convert.

* Jose Padilla (a.k.a. Abdullah al-Muhajir), the alleged "Dirty Bomber," was exposed to Islam during stints in American prisons.

* Aqil Collins converted to Islam while serving time in California's boot-camp system. He went to an Afghan training camp with one of the men accused of killing *Wall Street Journal* journalist Daniel Pearl.

To be fair, some conversions are shepherded by Muslims who practice non-violent beliefs. Still, too many are die-hard haters who consider America the great Satan who must be brought to its knees in the holy war.

In 1996, Sulayman Nyang, a professor of African Studies at Howard University, estimated that one of every ten African-American Muslims came to the faith through a prison conversion. Many of those being converted today have been told that Osama bin Laden was not responsible for the 9/11 attacks. Rather, Israel and the U.S. planned it as a pretext to launch an international campaign against Islam. Tens of thousands leave the prison system with those beliefs.

Strict belief in Islam is not the sole reason for all these conversions. Prison is a hostile environment for anyone, no matter how tough. Muslim inmates offer a perk which is hard to turn down: Protection.

Once an inmate accepts Allah and the Quran, and is identified as a Muslim, his brother inmates will defray the evil forces within prison walls from that inmate. That can quite comforting. Muslim inmates need not worry about attacks from other inmates, unless they, too, are Muslim. And once the inmate attends enough services with the prison imams and other leaders, he soon becomes brainwashed and readied for his duty as a Muslim when the prison gates are opened. When Muslim converts are released from prison with the customary $10, a suit of clothes and a one-way bus or train ticket, they know any mosque or masjid (Islamic center) will shelter and feed them and help them find a job. From there, he belongs to Islam for life.

During his twenty-five year employment with New York State, imam Warith-Deen Umar rose to become the most influential Muslim inside the prison system, responsible for the hiring of an additional fifty-six Muslim clerics during his tenure. He was the founder of the National Association of Muslim Chaplains. In October 2003, FBI Assistant Director for Counterterrorism John S. Pistole testified before a Senate Judiciary Committee, where he said that Umar and his underlings were responsible for converting thousands of inmates to Islam, some of whom have been drawn to al Qaeda. Mr. Pistole testified that Umar is known to have told inmates and his underlings (and assumably, fellow imams) that the 9/11 attacks against the World Trade Center and the Pentagon were justified, and that the hijackers should be remembered as martyrs, not murderers. Quotations are numerous from Umar that are ostensibly in support of jihad and the murdering of innocent Americans in the name of

Allah, yet he and fellow imams operated within the justice system with impunity. His power had been enormous. New York State alone now houses over 13,000 inmates who have converted to Islam.

After retiring in 2000 as chief Muslim chaplain for the New York State prison system, Umar continued working as a counselor in a consultant status. In 2003, the *Wall Street Journal* exposed Umar as an al Qaeda sympathizer and his contract was swiftly terminated. But not before he exerted tremendous power over thousands that would become future enemies of America while under the watchful eye of American officials.

The Department of Justice later learned that prison staff often observed Umar preach sermons that violated prison security policy, but no one spoke up or acted. Meanwhile, he was given "Excellent" evaluations. Many of the prison officials who hire and evaluate Muslim chaplains, are themselves, Muslim.

Umar, who promoted the Wahhabi form of Islam, is known to have taken four journeys to Saudi Arabia to study and receive training at the expense of the kingdom.

It is known, that Saudi Arabia has sent thousands of copies of the Quran to prisons all over America, and in Europe.

Just as with marriages to American women, American converts within prisons are of particular interest to Islamic jihadists because, once in the war zone (American communities) they are less physically conspicuous than mid-easterners and able to more effectively assimilate among the population without notice or concern.

Muslim clerics know the weakness of inmates

and are effective at stirring the hate pot, hooking blacks on the same old sell about being victims of white America, and how their ancestors were subject to two hundred years of slavery at the hands of the white man. Naturally, they fail to mention that Arabs were buying and owning black slaves for many centuries, long before and during the slave period in America, Muhammad being one of them.

In 2003, the U.S. Department of Justice released a report about the selection of Muslim religious service providers by the Federal Bureau of Prisons. According to this report, the Bureau had been far too lax in screening Muslim chaplains, contractors, and volunteers who work in our prisons. While these workers have to undergo background checks, drug screenings, and other similar tests, prison officials hadn't investigated them to determine their propensity toward violence or radicalism in the name of religion.

The Federal Bureau of Prisons requires that all chaplains be endorsed by a national organization made up of members of their own faith. Until recently, the Bureau accepted endorsements for Muslim chaplains and contractors from only one Muslim organization, the Islamic Society of North America (ISNA). But during an intensive investigation prompted by 9/11, it was discovered that several board members of the ISNA had ties to terrorists. As a result, the Bureau of Prisons stopped accepting candidates endorsed by the ISNA. No other organization has yet stepped in to fill the void. The report states that this situation "effectively has resulted in a freeze on hiring Muslim chaplains."

The lack of Muslim chaplains in the federal prisons system has created a need that also is often being filled by the wrong people. As the report puts it, "Without a sufficient number of Muslim chaplains on staff, inmates are . . . much more likely to lead their own religious services, distort Islam . . . and espouse extremist beliefs."

The prison debacle is another example of how government agencies have been turning a blind eye to the obvious.

CHAPTER FIVE

INDOCTRINATING THE CHILDREN

"Give me half a dozen healthy infants and my own world to bring them up in and I will guarantee to turn each one of them into any kind of man you please."
— John Broadus Watson, psychology professor

Autum Ashante is a talented poet and most charismatic. She has performed in theaters all over New York as well as a number of middle and high schools. New York City Councilwoman Yvette Clark called her, "one of the most precious young talents that this world has ever known."

As I write, Autum Ashante is seven years old.

She has acquired a huge base of information and knowledge for such a young age. Here are some examples of her outpouring:

White nationalism is what put you in bondage. Pirates and vampires like Columbus, Morgan and Darwin drank the blood of the sheep, trampled all over them with steel tricks and deceit. Nothing has changed take a look in our streets.

They took the black women, with the black man weak.

Made to watch as they changed the paradigm of our village They killed the blind, they killed the lazy. They went so far as to kill the unborn baby.

Yeah, white nationalism is what put you in bondage.

Wow. That's a message of love and peace if I ever heard one.

In March of 2006, the prodigy commanded white students in an audience to remain seated as she led black students of a "Black Child's Pledge", which began as follows:

I pledge allegiance to my black people.

... I will learn all that I can in order to give my best to my people in their struggle for liberation.

...I will train myself never to hurt or allow others to harm my black brothers and sisters.

Autum may be smart, but at seven years of age it's unlikely she developed this vast vocabulary and awareness of social history on her own. It's unlikely that she acquired a racist view toward whites because of any independent experience with racism. It's unlikely that she sought such information through books and mentors on her own.

While most little girls of seven are playing with dolls, listening to Beyonce' and partaking of a second grade education, Autum Ashante is being home-schooled by a single father in Mount Vernon, New York, and programmed with hatred and venom much the same as the children of the Ku Klux Klan have been programmed to hate.

As it turns out, Autum's father is also a member of the Nation of Islam.

When I watch a Muslim uprising on television

where hundreds of young boys are leaping and shouting and pumping fists and burning banners, I am acutely aware that it is not all their doing. It is the doing of their fathers, and their fathers before them, and so on down the cascade of cultural lineage, all in the name of Islamic fundamentalism. The kids are but an outgrowth of what has been ingrained into them since birth.

Years ago, particularly in the south, we saw film clips of small American children dressed in white sheets, standing with their parents along side a burning cross shouting disgusting epithets about blacks and Jews, as though it was a product of free thought. But it was not free thought, it was what their fathers and other role models pumped into their fertile brains until they could not think any other way.

Such is the indoctrination of Muslim kids around the world, and most especially in radical societies like Saudi Arabia where Wahabbist Islam dominates religious teaching. Their hatred is involuntary, and irreversible.

The Hadif is a book of statements of the prophet Mohammed which talks about victory of Muslims over Jews. It is taught to ninth grade, 14 year-old boys in Saudi Arabia. In it, this passage:

"The day of judgment will not arrive until Muslims fight Jews, and Muslim will kill Jews until the Jew hides behind a tree or a stone. Then the tree and the stone will say, 'Oh Muslim, oh, servant of God, this is a Jew behind me. Come and kill him.'"

Imagine that being drilled in the children's heads, day by day.

When one considers that there are but twelve million Jews in the world, and over one billion Muslims, it is truly amazing that such paranoia and hatred exists toward Jews. Yet, the obsession reaches far into the schools of Islam everywhere, so it's no wonder that these young people grow up as jihadists, bombers, rioters and haters all in the name of the religion of peace.

Also taught to middle school kids in Saudi Arabia:

*Jews and Christians are the enemies of believers (Muslims)

* The Hadith predicts Allah's victory over the Jews.

* The victory shall be for the Muslims because they are right and whoever is right is always victorious even though most people are against them.

* God grants victory to the Muslims if they have a true will, if they unite, hold on to God's Sharia, if they go by God's ruling, if they are patient.

It is the goal of Wahabbists to invoke these same teachings across the Atlantic and inside the borders of the United States and Canada, coast to coast, in proliferating numbers under the guise of religious schooling.

According to Mark Silverberg, author of *The Wahhabi Invasion of America*, more than 30,000 children attend Saudi-funded Wahhabi day schools in the U.S. where hate and prejudice is drilled into their brains daily.

In late 2002, The Center for Monitoring the Impact of Peace (CMIP) undertook a survey of Saudi Arabian (Wahhabi) textbook, the same textbooks that are used in Wahhabi schools in America. The results of the survey provided insights into the message the Saudis wish to instill in the minds of their students both in their Kingdom and throughout the world. Simply stated, Wahhabism either must dominate or be dominated.

The Report analyzed ninety-three school textbooks taught in grades one through ten, mostly from the years 1999-2002. In these Wahhabi texts, Islam is presented as the only true religion while all other religions are presented as false. Islam is the only religion leading its followers to Paradise, whereas all other religions destroy their believers in Hell. The Muslims are, consequently, superior to followers of all other religions, in both this world and the next.

Jews especially are presented as enemies of Islam and of Muslims. Muslims may not befriend them, nor emulate them in any way, lest that lead to love and friendship which is forbidden. According to the Wahhabi perspective, the Jews are a wicked nation, characterized by bribery, slyness, deception, betrayal, aggressiveness and haughtiness. As such, they have been a harmful element in world history.

In Wahhabi textbooks, Israel is not recognized as a sovereign state and its name does not appear on any map. Instead, all maps bear the name; Palestine. Peace between Muslims and non-Muslims is not advocated. Instead, the Saudi textbooks are full of phrases exalting war, jihad, and martyrdom.

Saudi textbooks do prove one thing as a certainty: Wahhabism rejects Western democracy, and embraces the regime of Saudi Arabia.

All this, while our trusted leaders embrace them as "friends."

In the right places, where vulnerability prevails,

children are also ripe for expanding the numbers of new Muslims. In order to gain converts, Muslims rarely impose on the well educated or middle class. They target the disenfranchised, the poor, the bitter, the angry young kids who are already brainwashed into believing everything that's wrong in their lives is the fault of the white American establishment. What better place to fish, than a fishing pond? Such is the case with juvenile detention facilities around the U.S. Recruiting Islamists are like drug dealers in wait outside high schools to sell their addictions for a more sinister purpose.

At least 125,000 juveniles are temporarily incarcerated in the U.S. at any one given time. While some Hispanics are also converting, most are recruited from the African-American pool which makes up more than half that number. From there, kids leave the facility and go about recruiting more converts at the bidding of their new masters.

Most children of militant Arab-Muslims in the U.S. are tightly controlled and indoctrinated by their elders destined to provide a grand service whenever the day of judgement arrives. They are like prized cattle, fed the same feed daily, closeted in stalls and rigorously imbedded with hate doctrines that will justify the killing of Americans and non-believers in the name of Allah. These children do not attend public schools where they learn reading writing, arithmetic and the stories of Washington, Jefferson and Martin Luther King Jr. They learn what they are required to learn, and that's primarily the Quran, the Quran and the Quran, with a bit of math and language built in. They are not permitted to assimilate within American society. They do not play with children outside of Islam. They do not attend movies, concerts, sporting events or American schools. They attend the mosques, and the Islamic learning centers. Period.

In truth, they represent a massive future army of hypnotized jihadists and suicide bombers, trained and equipped under the auspices of religious freedom, complements of the U.S. Constitution.

Militant Islam does not stop at brainwashing their own. Astonishingly as it sounds, the indoctrination of American students has now begun. While it is illegal to promote Judaism or Christianity in public schools, a federal judge in California has recently upheld a ruling to permit the presentation of Islamic thought to seventh graders. When irate parents first heard about it, they sued under the First Amendment ban on religious establishment. They lost. The pro-Islamists claimed this was only an effort at teaching world history and Islamic culture. In fact, it is much more.

Seventh grade kids in many California schools are now required to attend a three-week course on Islam which includes:

* Reciting Muslim prayers that begin with 'In the name of Allah, most gracious, most merciful...'
* Chanting Praise be to Allah in response to teacher prompts
* Quranic recitations
* Giving up candy and TV to demonstrate Ramadan, the Muslim holy month.
* Adopting a Muslim name
* Wearing Islamic garb

Twenty-five Islamic terms must be memorized, twenty Islamic proverbs to learn along with the Five Pillars of Faith and ten key Islamic prophets/ disciples to be studied.

ACLU, where are you now?

The main person behind the thrust is Susan L. Douglass, a devout Muslim activist who, according to author Paul Sperry, is on the Saudi payroll to introduce Islam into the educational centers of the U.S. For years, Douglass taught at the Islamic Saudi Academy outside Washington D.C.

How the courts have allowed this, is mind boggling. For years, Christian advocates have consistently met legal setbacks in their efforts to disperse bibles in classrooms, hold prayer and display the Ten Commandments on school grounds, based on the church/state separation doctrine. And that, in my view, is as it should be. Yet, the minority Muslims make such inroads where the majority religion in the U.S. is denied. Perhaps, Christians should learn the art of international terror and intimidation. That's a formula that works.

Meanwhile, by infiltrating our public school systems, the Saudis hope to make Islam more widely accepted and eventually convert impressionable American kids to their radical cause. I'm sure this is only the beginning. Massachusetts will be next. Then Connecticut, and then the entire U.S., unless the U.S. Supreme Court eventually rules on the case and shoots down the lower court rulings. If not, our American children are destined to be placed high on the Islamic brainwash agenda.

When do we ever learn?

"As the twig is bent, the tree inclines."
— Virgil, Roman poet

CHAPTER SIX

INSIDE THE MILITARY

While engaged in war against militant Islam, inviting Muslims to fight and assemble intelligence alongside our Marines, Navy and Army soldiers is like inviting the Viet Cong into the 1968 White House War Room. Among the five thousand in the military today, there are certainly good and decent Muslims who may perform admirably. But how are we to know which Muslims will put allegiance to country ahead of allegiance to Allah, when an obvious conflict exists between the two. The Quran is pretty explicit about that.

There are no neon signs blinking on the heads of our enemy which reads: "I'm A Militant! I'm A Militant!" Militant Muslims do not admit their orientation at interviews. If they have a more sinister motive for infiltrating the U.S. military, they aren't going to tell you. They look, talk, walk no different than moderates. They can be anything from a fanatic intent on killing his fellow soldiers, a Muslim chaplain counseling soldiers to secretly support jihad, or higher level intelligence employees who think nothing of sharing American secrets with the enemy.

Are the officials at the Pentagon and the White House living in Fairyland?

Any one of the five thousand plus Muslims in the United States military today may be a sympathizer with our enemies, ready and willing to carry out the will of Allah whenever beckoned.

As the U.S. was readying their troops for the 2003 invasion of Iraq, a black Muslim convert, Hasan Akbar, tossed three grenades into tents which housed commanding officers, killing two and wounding fifteen. Akbar was opposed to the killing of fellow Muslims in the war. Allah first, America second. He was overheard by fellow soldiers to say, *"You guys are coming into our (Muslim) countries, and you're going to rape our women and kill our children."* Akbar studied Islam at a Saudi-funded mosque in Los Angeles, but we gave him a uniform anyway.

Did anyone ever ask: How did he get that far inside the U.S. military?

Akbar is not just an anomaly. Many other Muslim members of the U.S. military have been caught in acts of counter-intelligence, selling secrets and weapons to terrorists, preaching jihad, etc., some of whom are spending time in prison today. Among them:

* Egyptian born Ali Mohamed, who immigrated to America in 1986 and joined the U.S. Army as a resident alien. While a member of a group called Islamic Jihad, he taught Muslim culture to forces at Fort Bragg, North Carolina. Though honorably discharged in 2000, he admitted being a member of an al Qaeda affiliate and pled guilty to helping plan the 1998 bombings of two U.S. embassies in Africa.

*   Jeffrey Leon Battle, an African-American convert, was indicted in 2002 for allegedly joining the Army reserves for military training which he intended to use to kill U.S. soldiers in Afghanistan.

*   In 2002, a former Navy reservist, Semi Osman, was arrested for allegedly establishing a terrorist training camp in Oregon. Investigators suspect that he was setting up fuel trucks to be used for suicide bombing missions.

*   Senior Airman Ahmad al Halabi, a Syrian born Arabic translator, was charged with espionage in connection with the detention of al Qaeda and Taliban leaders at the Guantanamo Base in Cuba. In a deal, he later pled guilty to lesser charges, including Lying To Investigators and Improper Handling of Sensitive Materials.

*   A Muslim Chaplain at Guantanamo, Capt. James Yee, was arrested in September of 2002 and charged with Sedition, Aiding the Enemy, Spying, Espionage and Failing to Follow an Order. All charges were later dropped.

*   John Muhammad, the convicted Beltway sniper and Muslim convert, was a member of the Army's 84th Engineering Company. Muhammad was suspected of throwing a thermite grenade into a tent housing sixteen of his fellow soldiers as they slept before the ground-attack phase of Gulf War I in 1991. Muhammad's superior, Sgt. Kip Berentson, told both *Newsweek* and the *Seattle Times* that he immediately suspected Muhammad, who was "trouble from day one."

Muhammad was admitted to the Army despite being court-martialed earlier for willfully disobeying orders, striking another noncommissioned officer, wrongfully taking property, and being absent without leave while serving in the Louisiana National Guard. Muhammad's charges were dropped and he was honorably discharged from the Army in 1994. Eight years later, he was arrested in the 21-day Beltway shooting spree that left ten dead and three wounded.

Abdurahman Alamoudi, the same imam who founded the American Muslim Council, created the entire Muslim corps of chaplains for the Pentagon which now has grown to over a hundred lay ministers, not including the many who are on the government payroll. In 1991, Alamoudi organized Saudi pilgrimages for all new converts with the blessings of the Bush I administration, and organized programs so that Muslim soldiers could watch Saudi television for religious counseling.

After the Afghan war began, Alamoudi was given power of attorney by several of the al Qaeda detainees at Guantanamo. Author Paul Sperry obtained tax records to show that Alamoudi's Veteran's Affairs Council is funded in part by the U.S. based International Islamic Relief Organization, identified as one of Osama bin Laden's favorite charities.

Alamoudi is now in prison serving twenty-three years for plotting acts of terror.

In his book, *"Onward Muslim Soldiers"*, Robert Spencer reports that in July of 2002, the U.S. Air Force asked for help recruiting Muslim chaplains for the Islamic Society of North America (ISNA), an organization with Wahhabi links. Many Muslim Chaplains were trained by representatives of the American Muslim Foundation (AMF) which has been investigated by the feds for funneling money to terrorists. Because of this system, many Muslim chaplains in the U.S. military are espousing strong

Wahhabi beliefs, which are indisputably in conflict with the mission of defeating Islamofascist terror.

But what does that matter? Such tolerance is being taken a step further in the U.S. Marine Corps.

Thanks to the efforts of Navy Lieutenant Abuhena Mohammed Saifulislam, a Muslim chaplain, and the standing policy of political correctness, the military base at Quantico, Virginia, will see the first mosque erected on taxpayer property by the year 2009. This must be greatly needed, after all, there are 24 Muslims on base. But it's anticipated, with a strong drive toward recruitment, many more will be housed there in three years.

Meanwhile, in June of 2006, Marine Corp brass, accompanied by members of the terror-related Council On American Islamic Relations, (CAIR) dedicated the first on-base Muslim prayer center as a symbol of the military's respect for the faith. (The faith of our enemies, I would add)

Lieutenant Saifulislam is the same imam who spearheaded the drive toward serving Islamic-approved food at Guantanamo for terrorist prisoners, instituted calls to prayer five times a day at the prison camp and dispersed Pentagon-issued copies of the Quran. The Pentagon gives the chaplain great latitude because he claims to be moderate. Well, if he claims to be moderate, he must be, right? They apparently overlook the fact that he studied Islam at a hard-line Wahhabi school in Virginia that was raided by federal authorities after 9/11, and he's tied to a number of Muslim radicals— including members of CAIR — that call for the downfall of the U.S.

This is like inviting a Japanese Shinto priest to set up a religious temple on a Marine camp in 1945

Iwo Jima.

Imagine, a rabbi demanding a Jewish synagogue be built on base at Parris Island?

Imagine, a Catholic priest lobbying for a cathedral on base at Fort Dix?

Yes, terrorism certainly has its advantages.

CHAPTER SEVEN

ISLAM'S PULPIT:
THE COLLEGE CAMPUS

In December of 2005, the *New York Times* reported that Harvard and Georgetown Universities had each accepted $20 million in donations by Saudi Prince Alwaleed bin Talal. This is the same prince who tried to give $10 million to Rudy Giuliani after 9/11, until the New York mayor told him to stick it where the sun don't shine. Giuliani was well aware of the prince's on-going anti-American rhetoric, and how he'd been denigrating the United States. His close alliance with the Palestinians and hatred toward Israel didn't seem to faze Harvard or Georgetown, especially when it comes to reaping the millions of dollars from Oil-rich Saudi Arabia. Little do they care how much anti-American propaganda the prince brings with that massive donation.

Many will cite the First Amendment saying we live in a land where speech is free, and government dissent is welcomed. That's as it should be. But is speech supposed to be so free, that we can allow pro-Muslim/anti-American rhetoric espoused by delegates of our enemies on campus during a time of war? These are colleges and universities where many students are provided government loans and grants with our tax dollars, while the schools happily accept whatever government subsidies they can glean. Is that not a conflict of interest, tax funds directed toward educational systems which give aid, comfort and support to the enemy of the United States? Something is terribly wrong there.

With a captive audience at their will, militant Islamic professors are using the liberal campus environment in all four corners of this country to spew an anti-American agenda and to recruit new Jew-hating Muslims. They do this with impunity, heralded by many as icons of free speech and dissent, with the full knowledge of faculty and government officials. Can you imagine, allowing Hitler's agents to spew anti-American hatred at Yale University in 1944? Or, allowing Hirohito to speak at Stanford in December of 1941, so he can tell all the students how terrible America really is?

Sami al-Arian, a Palestinian-born professor at South Florida University in Tampa, was indicted in 2003 for seventeen counts of various charges, from funding Palestinian Islamic Jihad, to extortion, perjury, murder and giving aid to an outlawed group. Al-Arian worked on campus as a tenured professor of computer science since 1986 where he was known to speak out often against U.S. policies in the mid-east, with particular venom toward the state of Israel.

Fact is, al-Arian had been under surveillance by the FBI for funneling money and aiding terrorist groups since 1991, but was never fully pursued until he appeared on Bill O'Reilly's talk show on Fox News in 2001, when he found himself under the gun defending two of his cohorts who were identified as terrorists. Two years later, he was indicted.

For years, al-Arian was widely respected amid Muslim groups who praised his contribution toward Muslim causes. He helped to establish a mosque and Muslim school in Tampa. In 2000, he helped G.W. Bush by garnering Muslim votes around Florida for his campaign, this in a state where the slim margin of Bush's victory meant the difference between winning and losing. Is it any wonder that Bush owes allegiance to the Muslim vote? Al–Arian was invited as an honored guest in the White House in 2001.

One wonders if Mr. Bush or the State Department knew of these comments, attributed to Mr. al-Arian:

"Let's damn America, let's damn Israel, let's damn their allies until death." Stated at a Cleveland mosque in the 1990's

"We are in a battle of life and death...against the Western hegemony and tyranny...what is needed is the dismantling of the cultural system of the West." Another speech to a Muslim audience.

"Jihad is our path. Victory for Islam. Death to Israel. Revolution. Revolution until Victory. Rolling to Jerusalem." From a video tape seized at his home at the time of his arrest.

In a forty-page manifesto, he once denigrated America as *"The great Satan which makes the wrong right, and the right wrong."*

In 2002, former federal prosecutor, John Loftus, filed a law suit against the Federal Government alleging that the U.S. knew this man was a terrorist for decades and didn't do anything about it. Loftus claimed that all of the money raked in for the charities was being laundered by the Saudis for several terrorist groups. Because they were getting tax deductions for terrorism and the U.S. government wasn't doing anything, he brought forth the suit. Shortly after, the raids started on Sami al-Arian.

The following is an on-camera interview conversation between Fox News' Shepard Smith and Loftus.

> Shepard Smith: You're saying the U.S. government was turning a blind eye towards terrorists who were sponsoring the murder of people, turning a blind eye, because of our quote "friendship and tax dollars." That is what you're alleging isn't it?

> John Loftus: It's even harsher than that. One of my friends in the intelligence agency said we knew that the Saudi's were laundering money through American charities but they were only killing Jews, they weren't killing Americans. Now, that kind of bigoted indifference all changed after 9/11. Did the U.S. know that Saudi Arabia was funding terrorism from the U.S.? Absolutely. They have wire taps for Sami al-Arian going back to the 1980's.

> Shepard Smith: And yet, he was a professor for a state university?

> John Loftus: He was more than that, he was an informant for the FBI. Why do you think he wasn't prosecuted?

This is just one of hundreds of pro-jihad professors teaching in our universities today. We, as parents and taxpayers, should be outraged.

In December, 2005, Sami al-Arian was acquitted

in federal court of half the charges against him, while the jury deadlocked on the other half. On April 14, 2006 al-Arian pleaded guilty to a single count of conspiracy to provide services to the Palestinian Islamic Jihad and agreed to be deported. In return, federal prosecutors agreed to drop the remaining eight charges against him.

As a thirty-year career cop and sixteen-year homicide investigator, I can tell you without reservation, that a not-guilty verdict rarely translates to an innocent defendant. Charges like that are not dreamed up, especially after twelve years of surveillance by the FBI.

Dr. Abdullah Mohammad Sindi is a Saudi Professor of Political Science who has taught in Saudi Arabia and at the University of California in Irvine, California State University at Pomona, Cerritos College, and Fullerton College. The Mehr News Agency, Middle East Media Research Institute and Worldnetdaily.com, have reported that Sindi has spoken out in support of Iran's President Mahmoud Ahmadinejad claim that there is no such thing as the "holocaust" and that "the holocaust is a typical Zionist myth", and that America will eventually collapse like the Soviet Union. He goes on to say, *"There is no proof whatsoever that any living Jew was ever gassed or burned in Nazi Germany or in any of the territories that Nazi Germany occupied during World War II."*

Sindi's teaching, interviews and publications are rife with Anti-American/pro jihad rhetoric yet academia turns a blind eye in the name of free speech while he poisons the minds and hearts of our youth.

According to his web site, Sindi still resides in Placentia, California.

In his book, *The Professors*, David Horowitz identifies 101 of the most dangerous academics in America who have been influencing our impressionable youth for no other purpose but to hate America while supporting and sympathizing with the causes of communism, racism and Islamic revolution. It is simply astounding that such learned discontents are permitted to espouse subversive propaganda on campus to thousands of students who attend college with the assistance of our tax dollars. Meanwhile, these denigrators of America reap the benefits of six-digit salaries and the good life this country has to offer. One can only conclude, if they hate America so much but prefer to remain, they are not merely teachers, they are part of a crusade to institute long range change.

Horowitz concludes that out of 617,000 professors in the Unites States, at least four to five percent can be considered as Anti-American radical activists who impart their individual brands of hate into college kids. That would equate to approximately 25,000 or 30,000 hate-mongering professors and approximately three million students a year in their classrooms. If only five percent of those kids walk away swayed by the rhetoric, that's 150,000 kids a year converted into haters of their own country. It could be more.

Unfortunately, these radical professors seem to exert more clout than we could ever imagine. The University of California at Berkley's 1934 *Academic Personnel Manual* states:

"...The freedom of a university is the freedom of competent persons in the classroom. In order to protect this freedom, the University assumed the right to prevent exploitation of its prestige by

unqualified persons or by those who would use it as a platform for propaganda."

In July of 2003, this passage was removed from the Berkley personnel manual by a 43-3 vote of the Faculty Senate. In it's rewrite, the injunction against using the university classroom as a pulpit from which to create converts to political, social or sectarian agendas, is gone. Following this change in campus policy, a radical lecturer named Snehal Shingavi initiated a writing course for freshman students titled, *"The Politics and Poetics of Palestinian Resistance."* In describing the course, the professor wrote, *"The brutal Israeli military occupation of Palestine since 1948 has systematically displaced, killed and maimed millions of Palestinian people."*

Is this teaching knowledge? Or is it teaching jihad?

Among some of the professors named in Horowitz's book:

* Nicholas De Genova, professor of anthropology at Columbia University. Being a staunch opponent of the Iraq war is one thing, but not when you tell three thousand students, *"U.S. patriotism is inseparable from imperial warfare and white supremacy...The only true heroes are those who find ways that help defeat the U.S. military."* Professor De Genova called for *"A million Mogadishus,"* referring to the eighteen U.S. servicemen who were killed in the Somalian uprising of 1993.

* Sasan Fayazmanesh, professor of economics at California State, Fresno. In his writings and oratory, this Iranian-born educator detests the United States and Israel, and denounces the U.S.

government's position against Hamas, Islamic Jihad and Hezbollah as terrorist groups.

* Joseph Massad, professor of modern Arab politics and intellectual history at Columbia. Massad has made no secret of his anti-Semitic position. *"The Jews are not a nation. The Jewish state is a racist state that does no have the right to exist."* Born a Palestinian-Jordanian, Massad hails terrorists as "anti-colonial resisters" for their sacrifices in murdering Jews.

* Professor of Persian and Islamic studies, University of California, Berkeley, Hamid Algar considers the Iranian revolution of 1979, including the rise of Ayatollah Khomeini, *"the most significant, hopeful and profound event in the entirety of contemporary Islamic history."* In a 1994 speech, he advocated jihad, saying, *"If necessary, we must go to the point of taking weapons in our hands to defeat the enemies of Islam...Let us also remember his (Khomeini) insistence that the abominable genocide state of Israel completely disappear from the face of the globe."*

* M. Shahid Alam, professor of economics, Northeastern University, Boston. In an essay written for the December 2004 issue of *Dissident Voice*, Alam likened Mohammed Atta and the al Qaeda terrorists of 9/11 to American patriots who defended themselves against the British at Lexington.

As a writer, I understand, and support, the practice of liberal thinking and freedom of expression. I understand that dissent is a healthy part of the learning process for it stimulates ideas and forces people to see more than one side to an issue. But it boggles the mind that our institutions of higher learning dare to employ enemies of our nation, when fine educators are available that can stick to their subject matter without indoctrinating our kids to hate America. I would dare to ask one university president to tell me what that accomplishes for the college, for the country and for the individual students. The money keeps pouring in from our tax dollars, which goes toward supporting this level of trash being spoon-fed to impressionable youths. The end result will be disastrous. Garbage in, garbage out.

Universities such as Georgetown, Harvard, Berkeley, etc. who permit such activity, should be stripped of all government funds which come from tax dollars, and exposed not as institutes of higher learning, but pulpits of hatred.

CHAPTER EIGHT

PENETRATING LAW ENFORCEMENT

As chronicled in the book, *"Infiltration,"* Sibel Deniz Edmonds, is an American citizen of Iranian descent who was hired by the FBI as a Farsi and Turkish translator one week after 9/11. The day she reported to the FBI, she was hustled into a secret room where other translators, mostly of mid-east descent were also awaiting orientation. She noticed several trays of cookies and dates had been laid out on a table. She knew that such desserts are customarily served by mid-easterners at weddings, birthdays and other celebrations. When she inquired with one of the translators, she was shocked to learn they were all gleefully observing the success of al Qaeda for murdering three thousand people in one day. And they weren't shy about their feelings. *"It's about time they got their taste of what they've been giving to the middle east,"* said one, referring to the United States.

This, under the auspices of the federal investigative agency that is supposed to bring the perpetrators to justice.

Following 9/11, the FBI was desperate to find

Arabic translators. Years of wire taps and surveillance records had piled high without translations. Until 9/11, agents were busy fighting organized crime, public corruption and other offenses, with less emphasis on mid-east espionage and Muslim enemies. Their Arabic capabilities severely lacking, they had nowhere to turn but to mid-easterners fluent in the language. The FBI publically claims that all the new hirees were thoroughly screened, but that has been disputed by a number of critics, including Ms. Edmonds. She stated that many were hired on without undergoing full background checks, while others started working for the squad — inside the FBI — months even before they were given top secret clearance.

Many Jewish applicants who were fluent in Arabic were summarily declined for hire as translators. While the bureau states they simply did not meet required standards, other insiders say they were concerned about assembling Jews in the same unit with Arabs who would likely object.

The Translation Unit has since become a focal point of many accusations of impropriety, espionage, disloyalty and theft of materials by Arab Muslim employees. It was the job of Special Agent and eighteen-year veteran, John M. Cole, to sift through applications and oversee background investigations of Arab Muslims for the Translation Unit. He uncovered a number of suspicious characteristics about one female applicant with strong family ties to Pakistani officials that should not be trusted with classified materials. Her polygraph test proved "inconclusive," which raised another red flag for Cole. He recommended she not be hired. They hired her anyway, and she is now working in the

Washington field office.

About six months after this woman was hired, the counterintelligence division was handed a spy case involving Pakistan. Someone had leaked highly classified FBI radio frequencies to Islamabad. They later determined that the only inside people that could have done this were people within the Translation Unit. The leak investigation is still not resolved.

Paul Sperry gained access to inside sources who told him that she has since become a major Islamic influence on the job, leading the way to installing separate bathroom facilities for Muslims, heading the Muslim Awareness Program and leading prayer groups. They've also hired her sons to translate highly sensitive classified materials.

Agent Cole, now retired, said that he had observed several lapses of screening and security in hiring translators, not limited to the one female. At least a dozen translators have major red flags in their security file.

According to Ms. Edmonds, at least two laptop computers containing classified information were reported missing in 2002 from the Translation Unit.

Any kind of discipline administered to a Muslim translator for breaches of security or misconduct usually ends up as a countersuit by the employee claiming discrimination. And unless those charges result in criminal court, they are inevitably dropped and swept under the rug, with the employee retaining his/her position. When it comes to divided loyalties, the U.S. government just doesn't get it. Allah comes first.

In 1999, Chicago-based FBI Special Agent Robert Wright claimed his investigation of Yassin Qadi –

later named by the government as a key financial backer of al-Qaeda – ran into a roadblock when another Special Agent, Gamal Abdel-Hafiz, refused to wear a wire to record a meeting with a Muslim businessman connected to Qadi. According to Wright, Abdel-Hafiz stated in his defense, *"A Muslim does not record another Muslim."*

Wright said that Qadi, a wealthy Saudi businessman, helped fund the 1998 al-Qaeda bombings of two American embassies in Africa.

This wasn't the first time Agent Hafiz had refused to secretly tape conversations with other Muslims. He used the same excuse in Tampa, in 1998, when the bureau was working under cover against Sami al-Arian.

Retired FBI Agent John Vincent, who had his own frustrations working with the same man, told *Frontline Magazine* that he never went beyond questioning Agent Gamal Abdel-Hafiz's loyalty to the bureau. *"It looks suspicious. We're all in danger. If Agent Abdel-Hafiz relished his position as liaison between the Muslim community and the FBI as it seemed and was scared of retribution, he shouldn't be in the FBI. When you're dealing with a Muslim, his first allegiance is to his religion. His second allegiance is to his religion. Later down the line comes his family and his job. I think Gamal was being true to his religion."*

Abdel-Hafiz was fired by the FBI in 2003, not for insubordination, but for failing to include information on his employment application that he had filed an insurance claim in 1989 after a burglary to his house. His ex-wife told the FBI that it was a false report, and he subsequently failed a polygraph. Hafiz countered with a suit against the bureau claiming religious and ethnic discrimination. The charges were subsequently dropped, Hafiz was awarded his job back in 2004 and reinstated.

FBI Director Robert Mueller has been an ardent supporter of religious sensitivity and has called agents to task numerous times at any hint of discrimination against Muslims. *"The bureau is against — has been and will be against — any form of profiling,"* he said.

Abdel-Hafiz is credited by some for spoiling the prosecution of Sami al-Arian who managed an acquittal of half the charges against him in 2005. Had he cooperated and performed his duties as he'd been told, a great deal of damning information may have been acquired. Now, though he was inside the FBI also doing al-Arian favors, he is still working there as an agent with access to classified information.

Not only that, the bureau is busy hiring more Muslim agents. Before Abdel-Hafiz graduated from the FBI academy in 1995, there were no other Muslim agents in the bureau. Now there are seven, and FBI Director Robert Mueller is busy recruiting more.

"We are recruiting Muslims as special agents," he said. *"We have been very active in pushing more for Muslim Americans to consider a career with the FBI."*

Just what we need.

Special Agent, Colleen Rowley, was working as chief counsel in the Minneapolis office for the FBI when Zacarias Moussaoui was taken into custody almost four weeks prior to 9/11. A year later, Rowley became famous when, in May of 2002, she wrote Director Mueller a scathing memorandum about the high level mishandling of the Moussaoui matter, which reached the news media. It's been said that her whistle-blowing act spurred the 9/11 commission.

Technically arrested for overstaying his visa, agents quickly nailed Moussaoui as a terror threat and found it highly suspicious that he had paid $8,000 to take lessons to fly a Boeing 747. Within days of his arrest, the French Intelligence Service confirmed his affiliations with radical fundamentalist Islamic groups and activities connected to Osama bin Laden. Agents wanted to seize his computer. When the request was submitted to headquarters to acquire a search warrant, it was denied. No reason given, but it was assumed that the public aversion to racial profiling played a part.

Months before the Moussaoui arrest, FBI Special Agent, Ken Williams, from the Phoenix office, had determined that a number of suspicious individuals of mid-east descent were taking flight training in the area for the operation of large commercial airliners. His fears that they might be terrorists were confirmed when they found posters of Osama bin Laden in the apartment of the primary subject. Two months before 9/11, Williams proposed to headquarters that the FBI investigate all flight schools in the nation for suspicious students of mideast descent. The request was turned down, ostensibly to avoid profiling. Two of those students became martyrs on 9/11.

No one knows for sure if 9/11 could have been thwarted had the proper follow-up been conducted by law enforcement. But the signs were clear and the information readily available for the asking, if it were not for self-defeating mind-set of political correctness.

Colleen Rowley went to retire, write a book and now speaks out often on the dangers of complacency, claiming that the FBI had been rife with roadblocks to investigations, policies of risk aversion, and bureaucratic paperwork that hampered the effectiveness of law enforcement. She is running for a seat in the U.S. Congress

In September, 2004, she told the *Minneapolis-Star Tribune*, *"Civilizations fall, not because of external attack, but because of internal rot. And we have seen a lot of internal rot."*

CHAPTER NINE

MANIPULATING THE MEDIA

In September of 2005, Saudi Prince Al-Waleed bin Talai purchased 5.46 percent of Fox News corporation. That makes him an influential voting member of the board. Let's see how long Fox will remain "fair and balanced" especially when they are duty-bound to report objectively and truthfully about the progress of Islamic jihad.

In March of 2006, watchdog agency, Accuracy In Media (AIM), urged a full inquiry into a report that the Saudi billionaire caused the Fox News Channel (FNC) to dramatically alter its coverage of the Muslim riots in France after he called the network to complain. Al-waleed bin Talai is also a friend of News Corporation chairman Rupert Murdoch. News Corporation is the parent company of Fox News.

"This report underscores the danger of giving foreign interests a significant financial stake in U.S. media companies," declared Cliff Kincaid, editor of Accuracy in Media.

The comments came at an Arab media conference featuring representatives of *Time* magazine, *USA*

Today, PBS, *The Wall Street Journal*, and other news organizations. The Saudi Prince's growing influence in News Corporation were among the subjects of a December report that had been posted at the AIM website (www.aim.org).

Journalist Danny Schechter, reported that Bin Talai gave him an interview in which he boasted about calling Fox to complain about coverage of the French riots. He said he called as a viewer and "convinced them to change" the coverage because "they were not Muslim riots but riots against poverty and inequality." And they did change the coverage, the Saudi reportedly said.

The Dubai-based newspaper, *Khaleej Times* concurred, reporting that Bin Talai personally called Rupert Murdoch to complain. The Saudi said, "After a short while, there was a change" in the coverage.

Another rotten seed has infected America, and we stand by.

Has anyone questioned the Saudi prince's motives for this huge investment in America media? It certainly can't be the need for financial growth, he is listed by *Forbes Magazine* as the fifth richest man in the world. It should be clear to anyone that the Saudi regime is interested in manipulating the nature of information that comes out of the mass media channels inside the U.S. The mere idea that the prince would call the head of News Corporation to adjust the truth in news coverage is a bleak omen for what's ahead.

Billions of dollars equates to power. We all know that power corrupts, absolutely. The greed inside corporate America, which also controls much of the decision making within government, can portend the death of America. Once the press is no longer free, and Islamofascism takes root in our information channels to espouse propaganda – whether covert or overt – we may as well hand over the constitution.

News media has become so sensitive (or should we say afraid?) to the militant Islamic menace, that they are deliberately failing to report information that may sound the least derogatory toward the religion. Such is the case in June of 2006 when seventeen young men were arrested in Toronto, Canada for plotting terror and murder by using three tons of ammonium nitrate as a bomb, three times the power that brought down the federal building in Oklahoma City in 1995. *The New York Times* report described the suspects as being of South Asian descent. Nowhere in their original story did the report identify them as Muslims, one of whom purported to be an imam at a Toronto mosque.

The one indisputable common denominator of international terror and infiltration is militant Islam. That's the way it is. The onus, therefore, is on the media to report what is, not what they wish us to believe. When the media is so intimidated that it no longer reports the truth, then we have begun the ultimate backslide of our free society.

In January of 2006, a source close to the *South Florida Sun-Sentinel* informed the editor of the JewishWorldReview.com that the Council on American-Islamic Relations (CAIR) was trying to muscle the paper into getting syndicated columnist, Cal Thomas, removed from their pages. Thomas has been a regular critic of radical Islamic infiltration inside the U.S. In one of his more recent columns, Thomas wrote about the London trial of a radical imam, Abu Hamra al-Masri, who openly claimed that Hitler has been brought into the world to punish the Jews, telling his followers they must fight for Allah with a mandate to kill Jews and other non-believers. Prosecutors say they found a ten-volume "Blueprint For Terrorism" in Abu Hamra's house, among which targets included the Eiffel Tower, Big Ben and the Statue of Liberty. Also in the documents, according to prosecutors, is an "Execution Section" recommending that Islamic agents be sent to any country intended as a target at least ten years before jihad begins. Abu Hamza wrote that suicide bombings are an act of martydom.

Thomas concluded his January, 2006 article, *"...political leaders (in the U.S.) repeat the bromide that Islam is a peaceful religion and that radicals are trying to hijack it. Are we being infiltrated by people who, on the outside, pretend to be peaceful and tolerant but inside wish to undermine and overthrow our government?"*

In 2005, Britain's Channel 4 cancelled a documentary about the abuse of girls in the Muslim community because police warned that it "might increase community tensions." The muzzle tightens, because fear works.

In February 2006, Muslim fanatics around the world caused chaos, riots, flag burnings and even deaths, instilling fear into the hearts of innocent people, because a Danish newspaper dared to print cartoon caricatures of the prophet, Muhammad. Had the outbreaks occurred immediately after the publication of these cartoons, we could subscribe to the notion that it was all a spontaneous outcry by devout religious factions within Islam. But the cartoons were published in September and the riots didn't start until February, nearly five months later.

Much the same as the French car burnings in October of 2005, this was a carefully calculated and executed plan, obviously orchestrated by a central Islamic command, designed to scare the hell out of journalists and newspaper editors around the globe. It's another ploy at tightening a choke hold on a free press. Problem is, it works.

Publications such as the *New York Times* and the *Washington Post* ostensibly declined to publish the images for fear of upsetting Muslims. Score one for terrorism. While our politically correct president decried the violence, he also managed to couch his comments with an indirect slam against the paper that printed the cartoons. *"Americans believe in a free press. With freedom comes the responsibility to be thoughtful of others."* Well, that ought to pacify the barbarians.

Ex-president Bill Clinton wimped even further. At a conference in Qatar, he chose to condemn the cartoons, comparing them to anti-Semitism. *"So now what are we going to do? Replace anti-Semitic prejudice with anti-Islamic prejudice?"* he said, obviously to placate the audience. One wonders how this man could make such an inane comparison. He went on. *"...this appalling example in northern Europe, in Denmark...these totally outrageous cartoons against Islam."*

Meanwhile, we didn't hear the ex-president condemn the gun wielding, death threatening, flag-burning bullies of Islam who have made Denmark, and it's citizens around the Muslim world, targets for jihad. Neither did he condemn the grotesque caricatures of Jews that have been published many times over in Arab newspapers during the past several years, including Qatar, Iran, Oman, Saudi

Arabia, Jordan, UAE, and more. Yet, we don't see Jewish mobs taking to the streets, burning buildings, killing, stomping flags threatening murder and scaring the hell out of everyone.

Mr. Clinton should also have visited the National Black Fine Art Show in New York, where a Harlem artist painted an upside down, Christ-like figure with a face that resembles Osama Bin Laden. What would he say if all the Christians in America started rioting, burning buildings, and killing people? Christians have been angered by other displays of art which have depicted Jesus in a vial of urine, and the Virgin Mary defaced by elephant dung, yet no one has been threatened with death over it.

The Danish newspaper, *Jyllands-Posten*, should be congratulated, not for the content of the cartoons, but for having the guts to stand up to terrorism by making a vivid statement about free press, and that no amount of terror or intimidation will alter free speech. Few publications in the world would have done so. Unfortunately, two of the illustrators received death threats and had to go into hiding.

While the boycott of Danish goods in the Muslim world cost Denmark billions of dollars in lost sales of dairy products, industrial goods, and others, Denmark's courageous and principled prime minister, Andres Fogh Rasmussen, went on saying, *"I will never accept that respect for a religious stance leads to the curtailment of criticism, humor, and satire in the press."*

The free world cannot allow barbarians with a seventh century mentality to start dictating what can and cannot be published in a free press, no matter how repugnant or improper it may be.

With systems of instant mass communication

today, it's a simple matter to rile large groups of young Muslims anywhere, whether in Indonesia, Bosnia, Chechnia, France, Holland, England, Scandinavia and of course, the mid-east where they are well-rehearsed at acting out in front of cameras as mobs hopping up and down, pumping fists, burning flags, and firing guns into the air. Considering the number of murders and kidnapings suffered by journalists around the world in the last ten years at the hands of Muslim extremists, it is no wonder that the media has become far more discriminating about what and how news is presented about anything related to Islam. Thus, Islam's greatest threat — a free press — stands on the cusp of censorship.

"Our liberty depends on freedom of the press, and that cannot be limited without being lost."
— Thomas Jefferson, 3rd U.S. president

CHAPTER TEN

BLESSINGS FROM THE WHITE HOUSE

Columnist Michele Malkin once called political correctness, *"the handmaiden for terrorism."*

When it comes to terror and the war, political correctness is the signature policy of the administration. And by following the leader, it is deployed in all departments within government, to the point that it comes first before the safety and welfare of Americans.

The President of the United States will not use the words "Islam" and "Terror" in the same sentence. Neither will any member of his administration. The government's constant reference to the "war on terror" is not only misleading, it is an overused phrase which is meant to couch the truth about our true enemy. Clearly, we are at war with militant Islam, not limited to al Qaeda. We will never win any war until we are willing to clearly define the enemy.

If ever we had leaders without foresight, we have them now. With the tone of tolerance set by the White House, political leaders, with rare exception, have gone to extremes to ignore the obvious and espouse militant Islamists as representing a "peaceful religion." That simply invites chaos in our country by people who represent an ideology hell-bent on destroying America.

It is unfortunate, indeed, that Islam doesn't assimilate as just another mainstream religion among the populace along side of Christians and Jews. But that is not the case. Rarely will we see Muslims at an American sporting event, or a musical concert, movies, or in restaurants like Olive Garden or Taco Bell. But they come out of the closet when it's time to scream and yell "discrimination" or "religious bias", hiding under the cloak of free speech and free religious expression.

Hundreds of investigative reporters, experts on Islam, former government insiders and officials and other valid sources of information are telling us what is happening, but the president and his staff continue to molly-coddle Islamic radicals, hosting them as honored guests, often learning later on that they had just kissed the butts of people who were supporting terror organizations. There is a plethora of information available on these seedy scoundrels, for the asking. Presidential screeners surely know their anti-American position, but they are honored anyway. Why?

In September of 2001, President G.W. Bush exclaimed for all the world to hear, *"You are either with us, or against us."* Perhaps we should be asking him that question.

In February of 2006, a firestorm of resistance surged from both sides of the congressional aisle — from conservatives and liberals alike — after the White House approved a $6.8 billion sale for control of six major American ports to Dubai Ports World, owned by and based in the United Arab Emirates. Duh! That is a Muslim nation who recognized the Taliban prior to 9/11. The UAE practices the Wahhabi form of Islam. Terrorism money has been laundered and traced to banks in the UAE. Two of the 9/11 hijackers were from the UAE. The UAE refuses to recognize Israel's right to exist. Ceding control of our most vulnerable ports to an Arab/ Muslim nation is like turning over control of the hen house to the fox.

In case the president hasn't been informed, the inarguable tenet of Islam is: Allah comes first! All else falls lower in priority. If it's Allah's will to violate our trust at the ports, our trust will be violated, without apology. Yet, all we could hear from the White House is how much the UAE is a friend to the U.S.

The mayors and governors of those cities and states decried the decision and implored the government to reconsider. Practically every senator, congressman and governor was against this, including the president's loyal constituency, Senator Bill Frist and Speaker Dennis Hastert. They all boldly stoodup to the Bush administration. Journalists from television, radio and the print media had never been so unified on an issue.

Finally, after weeks of debate and exposure, DP World withdrew from the contract, giving a breath of relief to Americans, no thanks to the administration who is empowered to protect us.

Our state of homeland security is, to say the least, pathetic. The borders are being overrun. Twelve million illegal aliens inhabit our land. The Department of Homeland Security has relaxed the rules and now allows some sharp instruments on board commercial aircrafts. Militant Islam has taken root. Our weakest link in the nation's security, where only five percent of the nine million cargo containers coming into the U.S. are ever inspected, was on the verge of being turned over to Islam.

The president was so adamant about sticking with the UAE, he threatened to execute his first and only veto ever since taking office. Now that's a lot of loyalty.

While the president lost this battle, the mere fact that he would permit such a risk to our national security remains inexplicable. Even to his most ardent supporters, it raises question of his motives for it does not appear he has the interests and safety of the American people at heart. That question resonates, "Are you with us, or against us?" A shooting war in Iraq does not make us safer. But preventing another tragedy like 9/11 does.

The Bush administration has to face up to the fact that Saudi Arabia has been — and still is — the main ideological and financial sponsor of Islamic extremism worldwide. According to the Council on Foreign Relations Report, that nation is the largest source of financing for al Qaeda, and blame both the U.S. and Saudi governments for not being tough enough.

Al Qaeda ideology is essentially Wahhabist. Billions of Saudi dollars are flowing through legitimate businesses, charitable front organizations, Islamic Centers, academies, private schools, wealthy Saudi individuals and world wide criminal activities for the sole purpose of promoting a religious philosophy that is antithetical to democratic ideals of freedom, tolerance, religious pluralism and Western civilization as we know it.

Until the administration confronts this reality in a decisive manner, any progress in the war on terrorism will be futile.

The history of the Bush clan's close ties to oil and with the Saudi royal family is not a secret. And many who are in the inner circle of White House trustees are, in one way or another, suspect in their true motives for how they are dealing with the nascent threat to the United States. Here's just a sampling of what I discovered while researching this issue.

The Bush family has been linked in a myriad of business dealings to the Saudi Arabian Kingdom for over thirty years. In the book, *House Of Bush, House Of Saud*, journalist Craig Unger points out that enormous sums of money have flowed from the Saudi desert to the Bushes, their friends and their business dealings over the years, amounting to no less than $1.477 billion. Unger lays out a compelling case that the Bush family is so inextricably bound up with the Saudi royal family that they could not be held responsible for the role that many Saudi Arabians played in the 9/11 day of terror, and the international infiltration by militant Islam since.

From the standpoint of an experienced investigator, it would appear that the Bush regime has sold Americans a bill of goods. By initiating a war in Iraq clouded with dubious justifications, they have diverted our attention from the major nation that supports terrorism because they don't want to attack their own business partners amid the international oil conglomerate.

G.W. Bush was the major share holder in Harken Energy Corporation in the mid-1980s when it sunk into serious financial troubles. His troubles were over when a Saudi national came to the rescue and bailed Harken out with $25 million and a seventeen percent stake in the company. If that didn't establish ties, nothing would. From there, Harken won a lucrative oil contract with Bahrain in the Persian Gulf.

The rest is history. The marriage between the Bush family and the Saudi regime has been investigated and written about by dozens of journalists around the world. It is no secret, yet the Saudis continue to infect the United States with their Wahhabi brand of Islam under the very noses of our government, with impunity.

It has never been fully explained why twenty-eight pages of the 9/11 Commission's congressional report were blacked out by the White House, censored, and side-stepped under the ruse that the information contained therein was "sensitive" and would compromise intelligence. Those who have been privileged to read the contents, including Senators Bob Graham and Richard Shelby, have stated that the information should have been released.

What did it contain? Damning information about ties from prominent Saudis to international terrorists. According to CBS News and reporter John Roberts, the redacted section lays out a money trail between Saudi Arabia and supporters of al Qaeda. The report clearly points out that after 9/11, the United States should have focused on Saudi Arabia, and not Iraq, to fight the war on terror, but it created the diversionary tactic instead. Leaks from censored portions of the report indicate that at least some of the Saudi terrorists were in close contact with — and financed by — member of the Saudi elite, extending into the royal family. The report found no connection in the 9/11 attack between Iraq and al Qaeda.

Why even have a 9/11 Commission if the salient issue — i.e., determining who attacked us, and who supported that attack — is barred from disclosure?

Alluding to Saudi Arabia, Senator Bob Graham, the former Senate Intelligence Committee chairman, said in July of 2003, *"High officials in this government, who I assume were not just rogue officials acting on their own, made substantial contributions to the support and well-being of two of these terrorists and facilitated their ability to plan, practice and then execute the tragedy of September 11th."*

Without going into reams of detail, it is obvious that the administration was in the practice of covering the butts of Saudi officials for no other reason but to keep the truth from Americans and protect their Arab buddies. Is it any wonder that the administration was so resistant from the beginning to see a 9/11 commission investigate?

Where is the outrage? Where are the so-called "conservatives" of the United States who bury their heads in blind loyalty to a president because he supposedly evinces "moral values and Judea Christian values." Why can people not see through the smokescreen? While fundamentalists glow in such "moral values", we're being sold down the proverbial river. The government has been playing the greatest shell game in history: Look here, look there. But don't look where it is.

Other than lip service about protecting Saudis from American uprising and prejudice, it has never been explained how and why the administration executed such an elaborate escape plan for 142 of his Saudi buddies within three days after 9/11, sending possibly tons of valuable terror information back to the desert, lost to the winds. This is war on terror? This is protecting America?

The entire Bush clan is immersed, one way or another, in the international oil conglomerate. Vice-President, Dick Cheney, who many consider the power behind the presidency, is the former CEO of Halliburton Corporation and still holder of over 400,000 Halliburton stock options. Halliburton is one of the largest companies in the world that provide services to the oil and gas industry. Just before the 2000 election, Halliburton received $140 million to develop oil fields in Saudi Arabia in 2000. Since, Halliburton is the major contractor involved in rebuilding Iraq and their oil fields. What a coincidence. That no-bid contract has been worth over $10 billion dollars thus far to the giant corporation, and counting.

According to one U.S. Senator, Frank Lautenberg, (D-NJ) Mr. Cheney's Halliburton options were worth $241 thousand in 2004, and rose to over $8 million in 2005. He still continues to receive a deferred salary of nearly $200,000 a year from the company, though he told *Meet The Press* in 2003, that he had no financial ties to the firm.

The multi-billion dollar Carlyle Group, is a private Houston-based investment bank which doesn't come to the public's attention very often. They are among the biggest American investors in the defense industry, telecom, property and financial services and are deeply involved in the war on terror because, among other things, they own the companies which manufacture weapons and vehicles for the military. Their chief counsel is James Baker, close confidante of the Bush clan and former

Secretary of State under George Bush Sr.

George Bush Sr. is on the payroll as well, as Senior advisor. According to one of the founding fathers of Carlyle, David Rubenstein – as revealed in Craig Unger's book – the Saudis have invested no less than $80 million in Carlyle. He lists a number of mega contracts between Carlyle-owned companies and the Saudis, among them United Defense and Vought Aircraft.

Is it not questionable that James Baker's law firm is chief defense counsel in the one-trillion dollar lawsuit brought against the Saudis on behalf of the victims of 9/11? Translated, that means a powerful member of the Bush inner circle is defending Saudis against Americans. Is it not a conflict of interest in American politics, that Mr. Baker's client list includes Saudi insurance companies, the Saudi American Bank and members of the House of Saud itself?

Few people are aware that Condoleeza Rice, the pert and bright Secretary of State who many think should run for president in 2008, was on the board of directors for Chevron Oil for ten years prior to being selected by Bush as the National Security Advisor in 2001. Among Chevron's business links to Saudi Arabia, are a fifty percent stake in Chevron Phillips to build a $650 million benzene and cyclohexane plant in Jubail, Saudi Arabia. They are also involved in a joint venture with Nimir Petroleum, another Saudi company.

Then there are the charities, like King Fahd's $1 million donation in 1989 to Barbara Bush's campaign against illiteracy. Why would King Fahd give a hoot about illiteracy in the United States? Or, is that but one of a series of back-door bribes for special treatment, which certainly paid off in the days following 9/11. Such may be the case of Prince Bandar's $1 million donation to the Bush Presidential Library in College Station, Texas. Or Prince Alwaleed bin Talal's half million dollar donation to fund a Bush I scholarship.

In Craig Unger's book, a by-line: *Did the Saudis buy a president?*

Though I have earnestly tried to avoid the perception that this book is a Bush-bashing exercise, it is difficult to conceive the gravity of the president's betrayal of our nation. I voted Republican in every national election from Goldwater to the first Bush . Regardless of party affiliation, people like myself try hard not to believe that anyone sitting in the Oval Office could be a traitor to the interests of his own country. But his access to inside information about the Saudi connections to international terror and Islamic infiltration in America is far greater than anyone's, and we all know it. Why doesn't the president know it? The answer is: There is no doubt that he knows it. The next question naturally follows: Why are our enemies being protected by our own government?

Truth is, there appear to be higher priorities than the preservation of America for our children. When it comes to Saudi Arabia, the Bush family's business interests and personal relationships take precedence over our interests as a nation.

One of the basic tenets of Saudi-American relations is that the U.S. would not poke its nose into Saudi internal affairs. Our government travels the globe demanding more observation of human rights from nations like China, Iran and North Korea, but say nothing to the purveyors of international terror and Wahhabi-Islamic infiltration while they still chop heads off in the city central after prayer on Fridays.

Something very familiar occurred to me while conducting research for this chapter. As a young investigator in the 1960's and 1970's, I studied volumes of complicated material and attended numerous seminars and meetings trying to unravel the connections between Mafia families around the United States and it's proliferation of crime throughout our cities and towns. At the same time, we connected the dots between cops, judges and politicians who sold their souls to protect crooks. Drawn on a chart, the vast network was like a massive spider web. They were not only efficient, but amazing, as a small number of bosses at the top managed to control the gambling, prostitution and drug industries. Meanwhile, mobsters invested in and operated legitimate businesses as a cover for their sinister activities, like restaurants, dry cleaners, garbage trucks, bars and hotels.

It was not much different than connecting the dots in the Bush administration to the oil industry, the military industrial complex and Saudi Arabia. The only difference is that the government is better at concealing their motives behind legal barriers and at the same time, maintain a successful public relations campaign for image and fluff. Bush lackeys in the talk media, such as Sean Hannity and Rush Limbaugh, continue to praise this administration as though the man walks on water. But they are not dummies, and they must see the collapse happening around us at the will of sinister Arabs across the globe while the president pulls our attention in other directions. Loyalty is often blind, and we hate to admit having been loyal to a bad element.

According to Abdul Malik Mujahid, author of *Muslims In America, Profile 2001*, Muslims voted in bloc for President Bush in the U.S. presidential election of 2000. Though no exit poll is available, three unscientific surveys of Muslim voters revealed that Muslims voted 70% to 90% in favor of Bush. In Florida, the last battleground, there would not have been any battle without an estimated 60,000 votes which Florida Muslims say they delivered in favor of Bush. Those numbers surged upward in the second election, after the president proved his loyalty many times over to Muslims, not only in the U.S. but to those abroad.

Boiled down, Mr. Bush would never have risen to presidential power had it not been for the Islamic vote. That may answer some questions about where his loyalties lie.

CHAPTER ELEVEN

WORLD EXPANSIONISM

"I walked down the street in Barcelona, and suddenly discovered a terrible truth - Europe died in Auschwitz.

"We killed six million Jews and replaced them with 20 million Muslims. In Auschwitz we burned a culture, thought, creativity, talent. We destroyed the chosen people, truly chosen, because they produced great and wonderful people who changed the world. The contribution of these people is felt in all areas of life: science, art, international trade, and above all, as the conscience of the world. These are the people we burned.

"And under the pretense of tolerance, and because we wanted to prove to ourselves that we were cured of the disease of racism, we opened our gates to 20 million Muslims, who brought us stupidity and ignorance, religious extremism and lack of tolerance, crime and poverty due to an unwillingness to work and support their families with pride.

"They have turned our beautiful Spanish cities into the third world, drowning in filth and crime.

"Shut up in the apartments they receive free from the government, they plan the murder and destruction of their naïve hosts.

"And thus, in our misery, we have exchanged culture for fanatical hatred, creative skill for destructive skill, intelligence for backwardness and superstition. We have exchanged the pursuit of peace of the Jews of Europe and their talent for hoping for a better future for their children, their determined clinging to life because life is holy, for those who pursue death, for people consumed by the desire for death for themselves and others, for our children and theirs.

"What a terrible mistake was made by miserable Europe."

— Sebastian Vilar Rodriguez, Spanish writer. 2006. (Translated)

In November of 2001, at the urging of the White House and intelligence personnel, Swiss law enforcement officials conducted a raid of a luxurious villa where the target was Youssef Nada, director of the Al-Taqwa Bank of Lugano. Nada had been a primary organizer and leader of The Muslim Brotherhood, an international organization founded in 1928 dedicated toward world dominion. U.S. and Swiss investigators had been delving into Al-Taqwa's involvement in money laundering and funding terrorist groups, including al Qaeda, the Algerian GIA, the Tunisian Ennahdah and the Palestinian terrorist group HAMAS, a close affiliate of the Brotherhood.

Among Nada's belongings, officials discovered a document, since known as "The Project," a fourteen page plan written in Arabic and dated December 1st,

1982. "The Project" outlines a specific strategy to establish an Islamic government on earth. Nada testified to Swiss authorities that the unsigned document was prepared by Islamic researchers associated with the Muslim Brotherhood. Simply stated, it calls for a flexible, multi-phased long-term approach to the cultural invasion of the west.

It includes:

* Using deception to mask the intended goals of Islamic actions as long as it does not conflict with Sharia Law.

* Infiltrating and taking over existing Muslim organizations to realign them towards the Muslim Brotherhood's collective goals.

* Avoiding open alliances with known terrorist organizations and individuals to maintain the appearance of moderation.

* Avoid social conflicts with westerners, nationally or globally, that might damage the long-term ability to expand the Islamic power base in the west, or provoke a backlash against Muslims.

* Establish financial networks to fund the work of conversion of the west, including the support of full-time administrators and workers.

* Putting in place a watchdog system for monitoring western media to warn Muslims of "international plots fomented against them."

* Developing a 100-year plan to advance Islamic ideology throughout the world.

* Instrumentally using existing western institutions until they can be converted and put into the service of Islam.

* Drafting Islamic constitutions, laws and policies for eventual implementation.

* Inflaming violence and keeping Muslims living in the west in a jihad frame of mind.

* Supporting jihad movements across the Muslim world through preaching, propaganda, personnel, funding and technical and operational support.

* Making the Palestine cause a global wedge issue for Muslims.

* Adopting a total liberation of Palestine from Israel and the creation of an Islamic state as a keystone in the plan for global Islamic domination.

* Instigating a constant campaign to incite hatred by Muslims against Jews and rejecting any discussions of conciliation or coexistence with them.

* Collecting sufficient funds to indefinitely perpetuate and support jihad around the world.

Sound familiar?

In October of 2005, Swiss journalist Sylvain Besson unveiled this document to the world in his book, *La Conquete de l'Occident: Le Projet Secret Des Islamistes* (The Conquest Of The West: The Islamists' Secret Project) It is a chilling omen, indeed. The information is known to American media, yet we hear nothing about it in the folds of the *New York Times, Miami Herald* or the *Washington Post*, not to mention television media.

God forbid, we should offend.

The U.S. Center for World Mission estimates that Christianity's total number of adherents is growing at about 2.3% annually. This is approximately equal to the growth rate of the world's population. Islam is growing faster: about 2.9% and is thus increasing its market share. At this rate, Islam will surpass

Christianity as the world's main religion by 2023. This is driven by the higher birth rates in the third world.

In an article in the International Bulletin of Missionary Research, Barrett & Johnson estimated that the number of Muslims would grow from 1.22 billion in the year 2000 to 1.89 billion by 2025.

While the United States is the big prize in the overall scheme for global Islamization, it is becoming a much simpler task among our allies across the ocean, particularly in Western Europe. The same principals are applying:

1) Assimilation and power through immigration — legal and illegal

2) Proliferation of mosques under rights of religious freedom

3) Infiltration of colleges and prisons

4) Periodic revolt under the auspices of social deprivation and discrimination

5) Acts of terror

6) Intensive public relations campaign designed to turn country against country, including the United States.

They're succeeding everywhere. Anjem Choudrey, a spokesman from a radical Islam group in England recently was quoted, *"We want to see the implementation of the Sharia Law in the U.K. Under our rule, this country would be known as the Islamic Republic of Great Britain."*

Great Britain is heavily populated now with over two million Muslims and growing rapidly. Some towns are as much as thirty and forty percent Muslim. London has not escaped terror as evidenced by the more than fifty innocent people murdered on July 7th , 2005, in the transit bombings.

According to the *Hindustan Times* in 2004, more people in Britain now attend mosques than they do the Church of England. Muslims have overtaken Anglicans. Figures released by British Muslim societies indicate 930,000 Muslims attend a place of worship at least once a week, whereas only 916,000 Anglicans do the same. Given such a rise of Islam in England, Muslim leaders are now claiming that they should be afforded seats within the House of Lords. It won't be long.

The Muslims of England are very diverse in many ways. But they do not assimilate into the British way of life. Rather, they demand that the Brits assimilate and cater to them. Their demands have increased for public education of Muslim children to reflect their religion, or official recognition of the Islamic faith. Native-born Brits are less than thrilled with their growing numbers and un-British-like demands.

Columnist and author Alan Caruba writes, *"Fundamentalist Muslims will not be satisfied until, from England to Russia, the whole of the European continent is Islamic. What the Muslims could not conquer in previous centuries, they have determined to conquer in this one."*

In 2002, a significant vote in France for radical presidential candidate, Jean-Marie Le Pen, was generated by a growing concern of native-born French men and women regarding the Muslim population and other immigrants. *"Massive immigration has only just begun,"* said Le Pen. *"It is the biggest problem facing France, Europe and probably the world. We risk being submerged."*

Seven million Muslims are the second largest religious group in France, more than half of whom are French citizens via second and third generation immigration. They are largely the result of France's colonial past, especially from the North African region.

"France's situation is particularly instructive," says Alan Caruba. *"For decades, the religion was largely invisible and Muslims represented the lowest rungs of the economic and social ladder, but, in the 1990s second and third generation French Muslims underwent a re-conversion of sorts, joining the ranks of radical Islam to seek an identity in a society from which they felt excluded."*

Today, the burgeoning Muslim population is changing French perspectives, where many have shouted "Bin Laden For President." While many Muslims in France do not openly approve of terrorist tactics, they seem to share Bin Laden's political agenda, and the inevitable Islamization of old Europe. France's Muslim population is expected to double in the next ten years.

Some attributed France's recent civil unrest as "anti-poverty riots by desperate youths." In truth, France is a socialist country where every citizen is entitled to free health care, subsidized housing, generous unemployment benefits and "living salaries." All of this without the need to work. Ninety-seven percent of France's Muslims receive such handouts. They are the ones burning cars in the street.

In Holland and Belgium, where Muslim populations are rising by the day, youth gangs have turned the streets of Antwerp and Rotterdam into arenas of fear and intimidation, robbing, raiding and attacking people at European cultural events and terrorizing shoppers. Algerian and Moroccan youths have attacked Flemish citizens holding an annual fair.

In November of 2004, Dutch film maker Theo van Gogh was murdered by a militant Muslim in retribution for making a movie, *Submission*, which criticizes the harsh treatment of women in Islamic society. The killer arrogantly stood up in court during his trial, saying, *"I acted in the name of my religion. Should I be set free, I would do exactly the same."* This sends a chilling message which stifles free expression of thought and information. Anyone who openly denounces Islam or its customs, risks death.

Responding to a complaint by Muslims, Amsterdam police wimped out and dismantled a street mural erected on the site where van Gogh was killed. The sign said, "Thou Shalt Not Kill."

Is it any wonder why we rarely see motion pictures, plays or television shows depicting Islam as it really is around the world?

In Spain, Muslims are becoming rapidly entrenched. Terrorist acts have altered much of their daily lifestyles, as they now live under the cloak of fear and intimidation. In Britain, young Muslims have rioted in several northern cities, and eventually turned the subway system into a target for terrorist bombers. Non-terrorist immigrants who do not openly support jihad nevertheless provide a vast underground in which the real terrorists — that is, murderers — and their supporters can live, operate and hide. As Muslims gain the vote in several countries, they grow as a massive political force that will influence policy toward terror and Muslim takeover.

Muslims are the third largest religion in Austria and growing. Largely political refugees, their numbers doubled between 1981 and 1991. The bulk are formerly Turkish and citizens of the former Yugoslavia from where the Balkan wars drove many Muslims to choose Austria as a homeland.

In the post-Soviet Caucasus, Islamic fundamentalism has led Muslim Chechens to use terrorism and war on the Russians to seek a separate and Islamic nation. The Russians have responded to the Chechens in the same fashion as the U.S. has to the Taliban in Afghanistan.

Several former Russian provinces, now independent, have large, if not dominant Muslim populations. These include Azerbaijan, Turkmenistan, Uzbekistan, Tajikistan, Kryghyezstan, and Kazakhstan. Add to this, Albania. The recent Balkan wars were largely religious movements by militant Muslims and, ironically, the U.S. sided with them and against the Serbs. So did the rest of Europe.

In 1980, there were one thousand Muslims living in Norway. Today there are 82,000. Norway has not been immune to street riots, attacks, demonstrations and political intimidation by immigrant Muslims, all of which is causing the nation to rethink many of their constitutional rights.

Some members of the right wing Kristiansand Progress party claims Hitler's *Mein Kampf* and the Quran are one of the same, and they want Islam banned in Norway.

"We are not the only ones demanding this ban," said Halvor Hulaas, chairperson in Krstiansand Frp to the local paper. *"This is an opinion that is well established in Scandinavian countries. We are now importing people with a religion that is practiced in the same way it was practiced when it was established in year 600. The freedom we have in*

Norway may be taken away from us if we do not start to have some demands to these immigrants."

Karina Udnæs, deputy leader of the Progress party's city council group in Kristiansand pushes it further. *"It is about high time Norway and Europe make the ideology Islam and the practice of this, illegal and punishable in the same way as Nazism."*

Some Norwegian leftists, however, are prone to capitulation and have suggested establishing Sharia courts for Muslim citizens. (Whatever happened to... "When in Rome...?")

Muslims in Sweden are estimated at some 500,000, or five percent of the population. Islam has become the second official religion in Sweden after Christianity, despite the fact that the Muslim community is a relatively new one, unlike that of other European countries such as France. The first mosque was built in Sweden in 1976. Today there are nearly one hundred.

In Stockholm, teenagers can be seen wearing tee shirts that say, "2030 - Then we take over."

In 2004, Swedish authorities in the southern city of Malmo were busy with a sudden influx of Muslim immigrants — ninety percent of whom are unemployed and many who are angry and taking it out on the country that took them in.

"If we park our car it will be damaged — so we have to go very often in two vehicles, one just to protect the other vehicle," said Rolf Landgren, a Malmo police officer. Fear of violence has changed the way police, firemen and emergency workers do their jobs. There are some neighborhoods Swedish ambulance drivers will not enter without a police escort. Angry crowds have threatened them, telling them which patient to take and which ones to leave behind.

Because Sweden has some of the most liberal asylum laws in Europe, one quarter of Malmo's 250,000 population is now Muslim, changing the face and the idea of what it means to be Swedish. Asylum seekers may bring spouses, brothers and grandparents with them. Civil servants say the city is swamped.

Bosnia is considered by many to be a corridor into Europe for al Qaeda. Nearly half the four million people of Bosnia are Muslim, for whom the United States fought for in the 1990s against a Serbian populace that was seen as oppressive.

But the history indicates that we may have erred once more. The Bosnian embassy in Vienna issued Osama bin Laden a passport in 1992, as reported in a Nov. 1, 2001, article in the *Wall Street Journal* titled, "Al Qaeda's Balkan Links." It said, "For the past 10 years, the most senior leaders of al Qaeda have visited the Balkans, including bin Laden himself and on three occasions between 1994 and 1996."

The Washington Times reported in 2005 that the Balkans are seen as terrorist training ground.

In 1996, a senior diplomat with experience in the region, wrote for *New York Times*: "If you read President Izetbegovic's writings, there is no doubt that he is an Islamic fundamentalist. He is a very nice fundamentalist, but he is still a fundamentalist. His goal is to establish a Muslim state in Bosnia, and the Serbs and Croats understand this better than the rest of us."

The story in 2005 is familiar. American military intelligence and the CIA have deployed hundreds of officers in Bosnia to track suspected Islamic militants amid concern that the country has become a refuge, recruiting ground and cash conduit for international terrorism. A decade after the end of the war in the former Yugoslavia, Bosnia has become a "one-stop shop" for Islamic militants heading from terrorist battlegrounds in Chechnya and Afghanistan to Iraq.

Not including Turkey, over 32 million Muslims now live in Europe, comprising at least fifteen percent of the population. Their birth rate is three times that of Europeans.

The Down Under has fallen victim as well. Sharon Lapkin is a former Australian Army Officer and a postgraduate student at the University of Melbourne. In December of 2005, she wrote the following for FrontPageMagazine.com. (Excerpted)

"In Australia, Norway, Sweden and other Western nations, there is a distinct race-based crime in motion being ignored by the diversity police: Islamic men are raping Western women for ethnic reasons. We know this because the rapists have openly declared their sectarian motivations.

"When a number of teenage Australian girls were subjected to hours of sexual degradation during a spate of gang rapes in Sydney that occurred between 1998 and 2002, the perpetrators of these assaults framed their rationale in ethnic terms. The young victims were informed that they were 'sluts' and 'Aussie pigs' while they were being hunted down and abused.

"In Australia's New South Wales Supreme Court in December 2005, a visiting Pakistani rapist testified that his victims had no right to say no, because they were not wearing a headscarf.

"And earlier this year Australians were outraged when Lebanese Sheik Faiz Mohammed

gave a lecture in Sydney where he informed his audience that rape victims had no one to blame but themselves. Women, he said, who wore skimpy clothing, invited men to rape them...

"When Australian journalist Paul Sheehan reported honestly on the Sydney gang rapes, he was called a racist and accused of stirring up anti-Muslim hatred."

Hello? Is anyone listening?

Could there be any clearer pattern as to the motives and goals of international militant Islam? Cannot we see the inroads they have made around the world, and what lies ahead for all peace loving peoples if this rate accelerates in the 21st century?

What are we doing about it? We are tolerant. We are politically correct. We must avoid criticism for fear of being labeled racist and prejudice against a religion. We must love Muslims, because they are so misunderstood.

Think of Islam as a huge tree. The roots are deeply imbedded in the mid-east, but the branches reach far and wide, over the entire planet. The leaves are budding and the flowers are blooming. Hacking at the branches will not stifle the tree. We must get to the root.

Writer, Peter Grier, recently published a prophetic article in *Playboy* magazine showing the undeniable trends which will cloak the west in a new way of life in future generations. It's titled: *Welcome To Eurabia.*

The U.S. is next. A virtual sitting duck.

Jihadists are becoming more vocal every day, boldly declaring their goal for replacing democracy with Islam in countries throughout Scandinavia,

Africa, Asia, and all of Europe. World War III is being waged yet we can't, or refuse, to acknowledge it. Imams across America have been exposed as two-faced, espousing peace and love before news cameras, then inciting jihad and violence inside mosques. Many insurgents enter borders with student visas, as guest workers, or under the guise of oppressed refugees, then turn on their host nations like vipers.

In Germany, which has welcomed "guest workers" from Turkey and the mid-east for many years, there are now more than three million Muslims, one million of whom will soon have the right to vote. The *New York Times* called Germany the "haven of choice" for terrorists who plotted and carried out the attacks on September 11th.

And so it goes.

Are there good Muslims? While I'm sure there are nice folks among them, they are but pacifists standing by while the final solution comes to fruition, shrugging shoulders. Muslims who publicly stand up against the movement are an anomaly, and they are at risk.

Not all 1936 Germans were bad people. But neither did they stand up to the Nazis when they assumed power. Minorities have often ruled majorities. All it takes, is cold blooded murder and the dire fear that follows.

Hitler's *Mein Kampf* was a deadly omen which went unheeded by the rest of the world. Osama has given us nothing less.

Our people — and our government — are sensitive to ethnicity, race, and religion, and that's as it should be. But when a mortal enemy disguises themselves under the cloak of religious freedom, that's when all bets are off.

It is amazing, indeed, that the nations of Europe and the United States have not the foresight to recognize the trends that will bring western civilization to its knees unless policies toward immigration and religious tolerance are radically reversed.

It may already be out of control. Ever worried about their political status, politicians pander to imams in the name of "tolerance", while Islam secretly teaches their kids to murder us.

The 9/11 hindsight commission rehashed the rights and wrongs of yesteryear in the hopes of securing our nation. If the plotting Islamics have their way in future times, there won't be another hindsight commission. We'll all look back one day and wonder why we failed to act on those ominous signs. Why we didn't see the obvious? Why didn't our government take substantive action?

John Forbes, a U.S. Customs official who directed a financial crimes task force in New York City said, *"It wasn't until after September 11th that we understood the magnitude of terrorist fund raising right here on our own shores. We were always looking to catch the big rats, but in looking for rats, thousands of ants got by?"*

Should Osama Bin Laden be captured or killed, the administration will slap high fives and announce a major victory as the media goes into frenzy. But in the long run, it won't make one iota of difference. Al Qaeda is like the Marines, they have their organization in place, they have their marching orders and a succession in chain of command.

Global terrorism will not be defeated with war planes, tanks and generals. We must reach those youngsters being brainwashed by the thousands to become our future killers, and change their mentality. It's going to take radical new laws, new ideas, intelligence, guts, and...that awful word: Intolerance.

In times of great peril, extreme measures are needed to preserve what we love. Senator Barry Goldwater was correct in 1964 when he said, *"Extremism in the name of liberty is no vice."*

Some folks prefer to bury their heads in the sand and believe what they wish. I see the world as it really is, not as I would hope. Afghanistan. Madrid. London. Jerusalem. Oslo. Bali. New York City. Once they take down the big prize, the rest will fall like dominos.

Barbarians conquered the mighty Roman empire. They saw it coming, and could do nothing to stop it. Are we there yet?

Lieutenant Chuck Harbolt had been right. Pay attention to the obvious. The Trojan horse is already here. And I'm scared to death.

Speaking before the Palestine Islamic Association in Illinois, in 1996, Abdurahman M. Alamoudi said,

"Muslims sooner or later will be the moral leadership of America. It depends on me and you. Either we do it now or we do it after a hundred years, but this country will become a Muslim country. And I think if we are outside this country, we can say, 'Oh Allah, destroy America.' But once we are here, our mission in this country is to change it."

Alamoudi was an honored guest by Presidents G.W. Bush and Bill Clinton <u>after</u> this convention. He's serving prison time today for laundering charity money into terror organizations.

CHAPTER TWELVE

QUESTIONING THE IRAQ WAR

"What I expected to see were grim, masculine faces... the image of G.I. Joe. Instead, I saw pimples and peach fuzz and eyes full of fear...The typical American infantryman was a kid."

- From *Pucker Factor 10*, by James Joyce, Vietnam helicopter pilot.

Americans invariably attach labels to people based on opinions, then they are pigeonholed for life. Anyone opposed to the Iraqi war, for example, must be a liberal. Those who favored the war, are conservatives. Nothing in between. Journalists and talk show hosts are notorious for attaching brands upon which the general population feeds and sings back to the choir. If Rush Limbaugh reads this book, he'll undoubtedly attack me as a flaming liberal because I oppose his president's "conservative" agenda regarding the so-called war on terror. What's troubling, is that people like Limbaugh are too smart not to know what is really going on in the world and in the U.S.

The war in Iraq, and it's aftermath in particular, gives cause for great consternation. With reluctance, I have found myself wavering on the fence between conservative and liberal, hawk and dove. I should never be tagged a "traitor" or "anti-American" — nor should anyone — because I disagree with the government's position regarding war, particularly one so immersed in controversy.

Labeling is impossible to avoid. But it is a risk worth taking, because the right to speak out is what the government is supposed to protect.

Celebrities such as Ed Asner, Susan Sarandon, Michael Moore and others are at the mercy of talk show hosts who set out to bend the minds of listeners by portraying them as anti-Americans. I don't believe that. Right or wrong, these celebrities are a deeply caring lot who use their notoriety trying prevent the killing of Americans and Iraqis. I think Viet Nam protesters — especially the veterans — acted out because they didn't want to see another American die in a political war which was simply not necessary. Some, like Jane Fonda and Sean Penn, have gone too far— in my opinion — and stepped over the bounds of patriotism and good sense in order to make a point.

We tend to lose sight of the fact that our young people are suffering and dying at the behest of the American government, under the guise that they are somehow fighting the war on global terror and therefore, protecting Americans. But when one delves deeper into the problem and takes a closer look, it's difficult to resolve how a pre-emptive invasion into Iraq somehow translates to protecting our citizens.

When the initial war seemed to be won, and

murderers like Odai and Qusai (Saddam's sons) were blown away, my first reaction was to pump fists like any good patriot. We were able to do this because we are the most powerful nation in the world with the greatest army. It was a war which we started, not in self defense, but in a debate over issues still unresolved.

When the dust settled, I could not help but ponder: Who anointed the United States as the police agency for the world? And what gives our country the right to invade another sovereign nation and kill their people because we don't like their form of government, or their leaders?

After all, there are dozens of other countries led by brutal dictators of depraved governments. Do we stop there?

Every time I hear Limbaugh or Hannity talk about how we liberated Iraq and now those people are now able to eat at McDonalds, where the women can now paint their fingernails and enjoy free speech, I wonder how they would feel if they lost their son or daughter so another society 10,000 miles away for those reasons. Because, other than controlling oil and perpetuating the military industrial complex, there were no other reasons.

Had America stood in peril from invasion, or our national security was seriously jeopardized, it would be a moot question. In the case of Iraq, our country was not in jeopardy of invasion nor was our national security seriously endangered. Why, then, are we sacrificing American lives every day?

My 21 year-old grandson is in the U.S. Air Force, now stationed in Afghanistan, and I am as proud as any parent. Should he lose his life, or suffer severe injury, I can accept the premise that it was in service for his country and in protection for all Americans, because Afghanistan was the root source of the 9/11 attacks. However, if my kid suffered the same fate in Iraq, I would be forever furious at the U.S. government, all because of a politician who pursued a personal vendetta, knowing he manipulated facts to justify it all. Please don't tell me these soldiers are giving their lives for their country. They are, in fact, giving lives for *that* country. And they are giving their lives for the Bush agenda.

As of this writing, over 2,500 Americans have died in Iraq since the war officially ended on May 1st of 2003, not to mention over 15,000 forever disabled in one form or another. That's when President Bush declared "Mission Accomplished" in a carefully staged photo-op aboard the USS Abraham Lincoln. The count is mounting.

So is the cost, much to the glee of al Qaeda. In a taped speech made on October 30th, 2004, Osama Bin Laden said, *"Muslim guerillas bled Russia for ten years in Afghanistan until they went bankrupt and was forced to withdraw. We are continuing this policy in bleeding America to the point of bankruptcy."* Bin Laden further explained that the 9/11 attacks cost the guerillas $500,000, while it has cost America $500 billion. We're still counting. The war in Iraq may backfire on all the progress we think we've made in our global war on terror, and go down in history as the costliest blunder in the history of American politics.

Weapons of mass destruction have not been found after occupying the country for the last three years despite the interrogations of many captured scientists and Iraqi officials. White House staff members continue to tap dance as critics from all sides emerge with questions about justifying the war. In truth, many experts — including American inspector, Scott Ritter — told us that the WMDs simply did not exist. But, why should a president believe what he wishes not to believe?

Talking the Iraqi war is liking talking religion. There are those who are religiously passionate about supporting the war, regardless of the evidence. People believe what they wish, and then support their position based on dubious facts that is convenient to that point of view. It cannot be compared to WW II or Afghanistan, because those were indisputable — black and white — issues. This one is blurred with a sea of gray.

In a pointed 2003 interview, NBC's Tim Russert asked President Bush an interesting question: "Is the war in Iraq a war of choice or a war of necessity?"

Mr. Bush was clearly taken aback, stammering, hesitating. (Damn, where is that teleprompter when I need it?) At first, the president said he'd have to think about that one, before he finally assured us the war was necessary.

Was it?

The administration has tried to make a case that Saddam Hussein had "ties" to al Qaeda. But that case has yet been made. In fact, mid-east experts around the world are saying that there had been no al Qaeda terrorist threat in Iraq before the war. But there is now. Have we thus exacerbated a national security problem, rather than defuse it?

Certainly, with a strong military presence in this Arab country, we established a strategic position to protect Israel and other interests abroad. But a haunting question remains, as it did in one other conflict in the 20th century. Were the citizens of

America — and the UN — manipulated into believing the war was justified while the administration pursued a hidden agenda? Did the Bush administration cherry pick intelligence data that supported their agenda, and ignore any information that didn't suit their plan?

The indictment of I. Lewis "Scooter" Libby, Dick Cheney's Chief of Staff, has unearthed a myriad of questions regarding motives of the Bush administration for invading Iraq, and more importantly, how the congress, the U.N. and the people of the United States were manipulated into believing the war was justified. As of this writing, the Libby case is still under investigation, as is Karl Rove, Cheney and others inside the Bush closet. For sure, the administration is puckering, because they certainly do not want all the facts released, as evidenced by the twenty-eight page White House censorship of the 9/11 report .

Books written by former Treasury Secretary Paul O'Neal and terrorist expert, Richard Clarke, clearly tell, from an insiders viewpoint, how President Bush was hell bent on the Iraqi invasion from the day he took office, and that the facts were skewed in order to make its's case. Clarke also tells of how the president immediately focused on Iraq — not Saudi Arabia — the day after 9/11 happened.

The jury is still out. However, the main question, is how much of our resources have been wasted on a non-threat, when so many more serious threats are burgeoning uninhibited, right here in America.

Never before, in the in the 215 year history of this nation, have we invaded another nation initiating war as an aggressor without invitation or provocation. We cannot compare Afghanistan, because we know that country housed and supported the enemy, therefore we were justified in invading. It clearly came under the heading: Provocation.

Contrary to WW II, Korea, Kuwait, and the recent conflicts in Afghanistan, there are too many doubts in the Iraqi theater. There should never be doubts when we are sending American soldiers off to die.

Our active military forces number over 1.4 million, not including reserves and National Guard. Hundreds of thousands of those... *"pimples and peach fuzz and with eyes full of fear..."* are deployed to, stationed at, or conduct exercises in nearly 120 other countries. Yet, we permit no other country to have a military presence here. I wonder how that would feel.

If we took ten thousand American troops from places we don't belong, and we stationed them along our own porous borders, we might do better at preventing terrorist attacks such as September 11th. And, by supplementing the Border Patrol, we would prevent millions from entering our cherished land every year, committing crimes, sucking social services, draining the economy as non-contributing illegal aliens and creating a huge opportunity for terrorist infiltration. The greatest danger to our national security is the fragility of our own internal systems and the corruption of government.

Securing our borders would make me feel a lot safer than stationing pimple-faced kids in some Arab country where people are systematically programmed from birth to hate us.

If that makes be a flaming liberal, so be it. I'll just have to be a proud one.

CHAPTER THIRTEEN

LIFE UNDER WAHHABI RULE

"Women don't matter to a Saudi man. Possessing them matters — matters crucially —but once the women were locked in and breeding, what happens among them doesn't count for much."
— Carmen Bin Laden,
from her book, *Inside The Kingdom.*

If the jihadists have their way, our children's children will be living in a Wahhabi Islamic society, much the same as Saudi Arabia lives today. Don't laugh. It's entirely possible. The powerful U.S. military machine will be held irrelevant, if not impotent if the trends continue. All the gleaming aircraft carriers, Patriot Missiles and F-16s won't mean a thing when the insurgents take control over the Pentagon.

If anyone dares to think ahead, there are numerous books and web sites which offer detailed information about religious and legal conditions (they are the same) for folks who reside in the Saudi kingdom.

Being female in Saudi Arabia

A woman in Saudi Arabia is a piece of property, much like we consider a farm horse or a hunting dog. While the nation's wealth provides stockpiles of expensive toys and technology, their social perspectives are still mired in seventh century mentality. Women have a purpose which is to procreate and serve their master, lest they face punishment. While the Saudis have softened their stance slightly in recent years in terms of educational opportunity, many feel this is a concession intended to enhance political image. They still hold strongly to the strict interpretation of Islam as practiced by Wahhabis.

A Saudi woman may be the gift of a father in an arranged marriage, where she never laid eyes on her husband until the wedding day. This is another area where the Saudis are liberalizing their rules – at least to the international audience — and, in some places, are allowing women to choose their own husbands. Of course, one wonders how a Saudi woman would ever meet a man of her choice, for she is not permitted to go outside the home unescorted without wearing an abaya, nor have anything to do with a man, yet make eye contact, without a male escort who is a father, brother, uncle or other relative. Dating, in Saudi Arabia as we think of it in the free world, does not happen.

A married Saudi woman will spend the majority of time in a home fulfilling duties with her children, maintaining the home and feeding the husband, not much different than a maid, cook or nanny, except that mandatory sex is included in the deal. When she is clean (not menstruating) she does not have an option of when, where or how when it comes to sex, for she is the property of the husband's command. Sex is her duty.

The woman usually prefers to remain within the confines of the home, because there is a sense of freedom there which is restricted once she walks out the front door where her dress and behavior is monitored closely. Many Saudi women who are born and raised within the narrow confines of the culture, will say they are happy and do not want any new freedoms, because they feel safe and protected by their husbands, brothers and fathers under this system. Bear in mind the power of cultural brainwashing from infancy.

Here are a sampling of rules for the Saudi woman.

*She is not permitted to drive.

*She may not vote.

*She may not hold political office, significant government positions or work as journalists.

*Outside the home, she is required to cover her entire body from head to toe in black (abaya). Only the eyes may be exposed.

*She is expected to start a family — have children — almost immediately after marriage.

*In public, she will eat in separate facilities from men. Same with public transportation.

*She risks arrest by the Mutawwa'in (religious police) for riding in a vehicle driven by a male who is not an employee or a close male relative. If the family has no driver, she must ride in a small, separate, walled-off compartment on public buses.

*If an ankle or a wisp of hair inadvertently shows while in public, the Mutawwa'in may beat her with a stick.

*She will not be allowed to leave the country (or

even travel within its borders) without the written permission or in company of her male guardian, which could be her husband or a close male relative like a brother or uncle.

*She is not allowed to go out in public without being accompanied by a guardian and one fatwa (religious edict) specifies that a woman cannot be in a public place with another woman; she must be accompanied by a male guardian.

*She is not permitted to make eye contact with another man, other than her husband, her father or a brother.

*She may not be admitted to a hospital for medical treatment without the consent of a male relative, or go to the hospital to deliver her baby without her husband being present.

*By law, daughters receive half the inheritance awarded to their brothers.

*In a Sharia court, the testimony of one man equals that of two women.

*A Saudi man may have up to four wives providing he treats them equally, provides identical homes and equal conjugal visits. Religious leaflets left in hospital waiting rooms, at wakes and on campuses tell women to "be content with a quarter of a man instead of plummeting into the jungles of decadence."

*A Saudi husband may beat his wife for disobedience, but only after warnings, and other forms of progressive discipline, i.e., banishing her from the bed.

*Husbands pay dowries to their wives on marriage, which is for the wife to keep and not for use in the support of the family. That money is kept by the wife upon divorce and may provide some financial security in the absence of maintenance.

*To gain a divorce (Saudi Arabia has a 50% divorce rate), women, unlike men, must prove harm or fault by the spouse, face the risk of losing custody of children, and be able to convince an all-male judiciary. Men may divorce without giving cause, by simply saying "*Talaq Talaq Talaq*" (I divorce you) three times.

*Upon divorce, women may retain custody of any children only until they reach the age of seven (for boys) and nine (for girls). Children over these ages are awarded to the divorced husband or, if deceased, to his family. A court can sever a mother's custody if it determines that the mother is incapable of safeguarding the child or of bringing the child up in accordance with the appropriate religious standards.

*The divorced wife can expect maintenance from her husband for three months only, after which she must rely on her family or charity.

*Saudi women have access to free but segregated education at university level, but are excluded from studying subjects such as engineering, science, journalism, and architecture. They are allowed to work in the fields of education and health but only make up five percent of the work force.

*In allegations of rape, a woman must produce four male witnesses to the crime for it to be deemed valid. Therefore, men can rape women with near impunity as long as they deny the charge and there are fewer than four witnesses. Worse, if a woman accuses a man of rape which she cannot sustain, she may incriminate herself. Is she is married, and cannot prove the rape, that will be considered an admission of adultery for which she could be sentenced to death.

*As noted in Chapter 2, a newly married woman who is discovered as a non-virgin, may be killed by her husband and little or nothing will be done about it.

G. Gordon Liddy, former CIA agent, Watergate figure and now a renowned writer and talk show host, wrote in August of 2003 how he happened to witness a stoning of a woman in Riyadh accused of adultery. Liddy was there on assignment in the company of another man who wanted to watch. It was a gruesome sight, indeed.

The woman was completely tied up and lowered feet first into a deep hole, enabling her to retain a vertical position with only her neck and head above ground level. (one can only imagine the terror in her heart) The execution ritual began with the first man throwing a baseball sized stone at her head. The woman screamed, pleading. A different man from the side assaulted her by hurling another stone at her face. She screamed again, this time, blood streaming. From there, spectators joined in and it became a public free-for-all with teenagers and men all taking their turns smashing her head with stones while she squealed in vain for mercy, her face now turning into raw flesh, bone and a mass of red meat.

After two hours, the woman was unconscious and her grotesque face unrecognizable. A physician checked for signs of life. He saw that her heart still was beating so the stoning was resumed until she was dead.

All this, because a raped woman failed to produce four male witnesses to corroborate her story, as though the perpetrator would be inclined to have sex with her in front of four people. First, she was a victim of the male dominated culture, and then the male dominated system of laws. Is it any wonder that reports of rape are rare in Saudi Arabia?

The peaceful religion. Allah is merciful.

In March, 2002, a fire broke out in a Riyadh school where eight hundred young girls were in attendance. The doors were locked, as always, to allow full segregation of the sexes. As the girls stampeded to get out, the Religious Police were at the door beating back their attempts of survival, forcing many of the girls to remain inside because they were not fully clad in their abayas. They also prevented other men, including fire personnel, from saving the students. Fifteen girls, all around 14 years of age, needlessly perished in the fire. Another fifty were seriously injured.

Stories abound concerning kidnapings and other acts of forced prostitution in Saudi Arabia. American women, including military personnel and other civilians, are strongly cautioned from traveling unaccompanied by males through the streets of a Saudi city where they are easy prey for Saudi men who feel it is their right to whisk a non-Muslim woman off into oblivion, never to be seen or heard from again, lost to the ages for sex, and then extermination when they are no longer useful.

R.F. Burton is the pseudonym for a man who has worked and lived in Saudi Arabia for many years. (Many writers use pseudonyms from radical Islamic encounters for fear of reprisal) He has witnessed numerous atrocities that would chill the bones of any feeling person.

Burton witnessed an incident at a traffic intersection where a white Buick was in the lane ahead. A woman wearing an abaya was in the backseat. Suddenly, the door flung open and the woman darted out. The driver, a large Saudi man, jogged around the front of the car. Burton assumed she was going to be sick and he was coming to her aid. Instead, he shoved her violently back into the car.

Burton wanted to help, but his companion admonished him from getting involved. Other drivers stayed put, no one got out to help.

The woman's abaya was unfastened, scarf and veil gone. She was a young, maybe seventeen or eighteen. She reached up to the sky and she cried, "Momma! Momma!" Blue nylon cord dangled from her wrists. The driver got out again and scrambled back around the front of the car. In a futile effort to resist, the young woman sprawled out on the road, stretching her arms out in front of her on the baking summer asphalt. The man pulled her arms behind her back and tied them to her ankles. Then he opened the trunk of the Buick, lifted her up, and dropped her in like a suitcase. He closed the trunk, made a U-turn and disappeared.

In her book, *"Inside The Kingdom"*, Carmen bin Laden tells of a Princess Mish'al, a great-niece of a king, who had been promised in marriage to an older man. Rather, she tried to escape the country with a lover but was captured. Her grandfather, Prince Mohamed, the patriarch of the clan, ordered her killed for bringing shame upon the family. There was no trial, no murder statistic. Princess Mish'al was shot six times in a downtown parking lot.

In 2005, a man murdered his own 13-year-old child. After handcuffing and blindfolding his pleading daughter, the father cut her throat in front of her two brothers and sister. He thought she was not a virgin. The father was a supporter of international jihad. No action taken.

Documented horror stories are endless for the female side of life in Saudi Arabia, as they are in most fundamentalist Muslim nations. One can only imagine what is not documented, what really goes on behind closed doors in the daily life of a girl who had the misfortune to be born the inferior of the two sexes.

The more liberal or compassionate of men may permit a woman to attend college, but with limited course selection. Those who are so privileged often take these courses, not for pursuing a career path, but as a respite from the boring rigors of daily life. A baby girl is taught the Quran, the Quran and the Quran, and brainwashed every day by her mother or older females that it is her duty to serve the men, to obey the men, and to give them what they demand. Any deviance from such servitude can — at the whim of her guardian or the Religious Police — render her severely and brutally punished. She walks every step of her life knowing this.

Sharia law

This is the law as interpreted by Wahhabi Muslims and/or spelled out in the Quran. It is the form of governing laws that Wahhabists in Europe, Africa Asia and the United States have openly promised to enact when the final takeover is complete. They see this, not as an effort, but a promise and a destination that will be fulfilled by Allah.

Public records (numbers of undocumented incidents are unknown) tell us that the Saudi government beheaded 52 men and one woman in 2004 for crimes including murder, homosexuality, armed robbery and drug trafficking. The Saudis say such punishment is sanctioned by Islamic tradition. (This does not include stonings and state-ignored killings for family honor)

State-ordered beheadings are performed in courtyards outside crowded mosques in major cities after weekly Friday prayer services. A condemned convict is brought into the courtyard, hands tied, and forced to bow before an executioner, who swings a huge sword amid cries from onlookers of "Allah Akbar!" Arabic for "God is great."

In April of 2005, R. F. Burton was invited by a Saudi to view a beheading at Chop Chop Square, next to the mosque in Deerah, but after listening to another friend's account of one he had attended, he nearly changed his mind.

After noon prayer, a police van holding the prisoner pulled up in Chop Chop Square where a crowd had formed in great anticipation. The prisoner—drugged, cuffed, barefoot, manacled, and blindfolded—was led from the van by a police officer to the center of the square and made to kneel down, facing Mecca, the holy city. A minor official from the Interior Ministry read out the charges against the kneeling prisoner. The executioner—a large black man with a scimitar — approached the kneeling prisoner from behind. After the sentence was read, the executioner jabbed the prisoner in the lower back with the tip of the sword, causing the prisoner to involuntarily jerk up. When he did, the sword flashed down. At that moment the head was sliced off and sent flying across the square. Blood jets from severed arteries and jugular veins, sprayed into the air like a fountain. The frenzied crowd screamed in unison, "Allah Akbar!"

In another execution, it was described that the prisoner jerked funny when jabbed in the back, and the blade glanced off his shoulder and only cut through half his neck. After falling over sideways, blood squirted like a geyser from the gash in his neck. The prisoner moaned. It took two more swings to hack his head off. When it was over, a doctor walked over to the body and check his pulse. (of a headless body?) The prisoner was executed for smuggling narcotics. It has been said, but unconfirmed, that it is part of the executioner's ritual to use three whacks, the first to inflict pain and terror, the second to nearly sever and the third to finish.

That same year, the *Arab Gazette* reported that Zayid Bin Ali Bin Saleh Al-Thabiti had been beheaded for practicing sorcery and magic.

Saudi Arabia uses public beheading as the punishment for murder, rape, drug trafficking, apostasy (turning your back on your religion, in this case, Islam) and sometimes for other offenses, such as practicing witchcraft, highway robbery and homosexuality. While the King has the final say in commuting the death penalty imposed by a judge, the victim's family can pardon the accused at any time, which happens on occasion even minutes before the executioner delivers the death blow.

Imprisonment, flogging (administered by a man who holds the Quran, under his arm to prevent him from lifting the arm too high) and amputation (of the right hand, or cross amputation of the right hand and left foot) are for other offenses, as the judge deems fit.

Married people — most always women — convicted of adultery may be executed by stoning. And in what are deemed by the authorities as very serious criminal cases involving violence, the person executed may be crucified afterwards.

In April of 2005, three Saudis were beheaded then pinned to a crucifix, their chopped-off heads placed on top of the pole for all to gawk at. The three were found guilty of kidnapping, robbery, murder, and shooting police, high officials, imams and judges in the Al Jouf region.

In December of 2005, The Greater Shari'a Court of Dammam sentenced Puthan Veettil 'Abd ul-Latif Noushad, an Indian citizen, to be punished by having his right eye gouged out in retribution for his role in a brawl in April 2003 in which a Saudi citizen was injured. A court of appeal in Riyadh reportedly asked whether the Saudi man would accept monetary compensation instead.

"This literal eye-for-an-eye sentence is torture masquerading as justice," said Joe Stork, deputy director of Human Rights Watch's Middle East division.

Saudi Arabia acceded to the Convention Against Torture in 1997. However, Noushad's case is the third known instance in 2005 in which a Saudi court has issued a sentence of eye-gouging, according to the Human Rights Watch.

One common denominator I found in researching the issue of grotesque punishment in Saudi Arabia is that they are invariably conducted as a public spectacle, where blood-thirsty observers, children included, root and cheer as though at a sporting event. There appears to be a morbid fascination for watching death in motion.

While some may argue that Saudi Arabia's system results in a lower rate of crime compared to the U.S., I seriously doubt we would ever want to live under a government that is so arbitrary. Many observers suggest that criminal justice figures reported by the Saudi Kingdom are skewed and should be viewed with a jaundiced eye. In a closed society, it would be a simple matter, indeed, to record any figure they wish, whether it be incidents of murder or numbers of executions.

Criminal cases in Saudi Arabia are heard by the General Sharia (or Islamic court). The last stage of judical review is by the Supreme Judical Council. This eleven-member body reviews judgements handed down in major cases. In cases of capital punishment the sentence needs to be approved by the Royal court. Sharia is known as "the word of God" and is based upon the Quran.

Many laws are vaguely worded which means individuals can be arrested and imprisoned on religious or political grounds. Carrying a Christian bible in public can land someone in prison for many years. Once arrested, detainees are usually held incommunicado and are denied any contact with family members or lawyers. Some prisoners have stated that they were forced to sign false confessions. According to prisoner accounts, torture methods have included electric shock, cigarette burns, nail-pulling, beatings and threats to family members. Some prisoners have died as a result.

Prisoners frequently know nothing about the status of their cases, do not attend their trials and often are not even informed when they have been convicted. This adds to the suffering because many have no idea why or how long they will be in jail or whether they face execution. Court hearings are held in secret which means that the families of the defendants as well as the general public are denied the right to be present. The hearings last between five minutes and two hours, even for the most serious cases. Defendants have no right to a lawyer and have little opportunity to mount a defense. Many are denied the right to call witnesses and evidence that may have been gathered during the investigation is hidden from the defendant. The judge acts as the defendant's lawyer and questions the prosecution. According to Amnesty International while some laws in Saudi Arabia refer to detainees having lawyers, it is rare. Defendants can be convicted solely on the basis of confessions which may have been extracted by torture.

While Saudi Arabia is deeply involved in world affairs via the oil channel, there is no concentrated effort among the free nations of the world – United States in particular — to hold them accountable to the mere concept of human rights. The UN admonished Saddam Hussein and other despots of the world for barbaric acts against humanity, but Saudi Arabia is coated with Teflon, as though they have virtually bribed the globe into a state of immunity from inspection, immunity from sanctions and immunity from criticism. Because they hold the wealth, our government representatives kiss their barbarian butts.

"The only difference between Saudi Islam and that of the ultra-hard-line Afghan Taliban is the opulence and private self-indulgence of the al-Sauds. The Saudis are the Taliban in luxury."

— Carmen Bin Laden, from her book, *Inside The Kingdom.*

Carmen bin Laden was married for twenty years to the brother of Osama bin Laden.

CHAPTER FOURTEEN

THE DARK CRYSTAL BALL

Forecasting The Future

Think of Radical Islam as tracking a huge killer epidemic festering in the far distance, while we wonder if it's going to come our way and ravage our lives, or if it's going to veer off in another direction. We, in the United States, have never been subject to such devastation. It always happens somewhere else. Do we wait and watch, like imbeciles, until it is upon us? Or do we take some kind of action in advance — before the point of no return — to thwart off the deadly onslaught?

If we do not alter our strategy for this "disease", it will be here before we know it. But it's not a disease that will visibly invade, like a swarm of locusts or killer bees. They will root inside the land right under our noses, just like the aliens in *War Of The Worlds*, where they will grow stronger and more prosperous and finally, ubiquitous until the time is right. That's when the all-out invasion will catch a weakened United States by surprise, and we'll be scratching heads — whatever heads are left.

If our nation's leaders continue to handle the militant Islamic problem in a similar manner as the Bush I, Clinton and Bush II administrations, I predict a time table of about one hundred years before Islam is dominant in North America. All those who are non-believers, our grandchildren and their kids, will be relegated to a life equaling hell on earth.

The following scenarios are presented as realistic possibilities of how future conditions in the United States will be changed if the trend continues unabated.

2016 — Ten Years From Today

The slope gets slippery.

Osama bin Laden may be dead or captured, but either way it won't matter because his top lieutenant has taken over in his place. Bin Laden's martyrdom is a guiding beacon for the cause of Islamic jihad, emboldening the enemy into a more fanatical and determined force.

Incidents of terror have accelerated around the country, including two or three major attacks on national landmarks, entertainment and transportation centers. Among these; the tunnel system in New York City, a major bridge, Statue of Liberty, and Disneyworld. Al-Qaeda accepts responsibility for the attacks. Muslims throughout America and the world claim it is the fault of the American government because of their policies toward Islam.

A small number of suicide bombers have begun their rain of terror in selected cities where restaurants, bus stations, airport terminals and police stations are targeted. Bombers are American Muslims, mostly blacks, Hispanics and Caucasians who are the product of inter-racial marriage with Arabs during the 1990s, who easily assimilate within American society without notice.

Arab Muslim organizations step up protests and law suits against those who they say are practicing discrimination against their religion. Government is gripped with fear of confronting, combating, criticizing or even identifying Islamic fund-amentalists as our enemy.

Mired in ignorance and complacency, American voters have elected people into office based on their personality, charisma and "high religious and moral values." Thus, more of the same, ineffective leadership. Worried now of losing a major voting block, the president refuses to denounce Muslims, in general, and continues to tell Americans that Islam is a peaceful religion and that only a radical faction is causing all the problems. He/she keeps inviting Muslims clerics as honored guests to the White House who later become indicted for financing terrorism. The FBI, CIA and NSA are rife with scandals concerning traitorous espionage within the agencies.

The travel and theme park industries experience huge declines due to fears of more Islamic terror, thus affecting the national economy in which interest rates are zooming higher than ever. Public sentiment and some vocal rogue politicians who speak out against Saudi Arabia causes OPEC to raise crude oil prices to a point where gasoline is over eight dollars a gallon. As a result, the rising cost of commodities are passed on to the consumer and inflation soars. The unemployment rate soars to fifteen percent.

Using our bases in Iraq, we wage a military war

against Iran after learning that the fundamentalist Shiite state has acquired nuclear weapons and intend on using them against Israel, and other nations. Our National Guard and army forces are spread so thin, that it becomes necessary to re-institute the draft as the all-volunteer military no longer supplies the manpower needed to deploy forces in the mid-east and Afghanistan where guerilla insurgents continue to wreak havoc with American forces. Thousands more lives are lost every year. All coalition countries have backed out of assisting the U.S., with the exception of the UK and Australia.

Meanwhile, small bands of Arab/Islamic gangs are attacking "non-believers" of various major cities, particularly Los Angeles, New York, Chicago, Detroit and Tampa. Bodies are found beheaded. Police departments are overwhelmed and undermanned. Half the National Guard is overseas fighting other wars and unable to protect its citizens on the domestic front.

A private, well-armed American militia has swelled into a small army of its own, patrolling streets of urbania and other targets of Islamic terrorism. Numbers of shootings and killings of Arab youths increase which backfires and triggers more protests and outrage among the Muslim community. While the militia seem to win some battles, they cannot win the war. To the delight of militant Islamics, many Americans are prosecuted by the federal government for hate crimes and violations of civil rights. Citizens are behind bars for trying to protect America, while the enemy roams free.

The ACLU continues to champion freedoms of speech and religion on behalf of Islamic groups, defending several insurgents who claim harassment from the U.S. government. With the rising impact of Islamic radicalism, conservative America draws together against the ACLU in protests across the nation. Militia vigilante groups are credited with the random killings of two or three ACLU lawyers. Their ranks diminish as attorneys become more afraid.

In-fighting between right wing and left wing Americans spill into the streets with civil disturbances, demonstrations and racial disharmony. Feeding off the rise in paranoia, urban gangs enter into the mix, stepping up violence and making demands upon government resources.

Al-Jazeera, the Arab news network, applies for a license to operate as an American company based in a major city with national affiliates. The FCC denies the application, but lawmakers are at odds over accusations that they are violating free speech, press and religion. Meanwhile, outspoken comment-ators critical of Islmofascist inroads within the U.S., such as Bill O'Reilly, Lou Dobbs and Michael Savage, have severed their contracts and crossed over to different networks because of back-door arm-twisting by corporate executives in an attempt to tone down the anti-Muslim rhetoric. One well-known television commentator is found murdered in his home, along with his entire family. This has a profound impact on future stories from other television journalists.

Funded mostly by Saudi Arabia, another two thousand mosques and learning centers have sprouted up in all fifty states, with primary focus on cities with a high concentration of African-Americans, i.e. Detroit, Camden, Atlanta, Boston, Houston, Milwaukee and Chicago. Posing as houses of worship, these facilities are virtual war-rooms and planning centers for financial support, arms and fountains of propaganda. Some suburban towns in the northeast and mid-west are nearly all Muslim and congressional districts vote several Muslims into the U.S. House of Representatives.

Borders with Mexico are tightened by construction of a 700-mile wall, and by enforcement against American businesses that knowingly employ illegal aliens. But it is too late. The insurgency is now rooted deep inside the fabric of United States.

A small coalition of politicians propose a constitutional amendment to narrow the scope of First Amendment freedoms to our enemies, particular as they relate to religion, stating that such freedom is being exploited as their strongest weapon. The amendment would be reworded: "...freedom of religion, provided that no religion is used as subterfuge by an enemy actively at war to overthrow the U.S. government." The ACLU, religious right and celebrity groups fight the proposal, which is soundly defeated in the senate.

Lawmakers bow to pressure from Christian fundamentalists to allow bibles in the classrooms of public schools. They, the fundamentalists, will claim that faith in Jesus and prayer will solve the problems facing the nation. A fundamentalist-loaded Supreme Court upholds the ruling. As a result, Muslims take to the streets and demand equal recognition by installing the Quran in all public facilities, buildings and classrooms.

Whatever action/inaction the government has taken, all is worse, not better. The nation is on the brink of chaos, and al-Qaeda is basking in every minute of it. The grand plan of jihad is working. The irony is that it has mostly been funded, by proxy, from the American dollar.

2046 — Forty Years From Today

Point of no return?

Two presidents, one vice-president and a number of congressmen have been assassinated by militant Muslims in the last thirty years. Most of the congressmen were vocal opponents of Islam who proposed a declaration of war against Saudi Arabia after it was learned that they have been financing international jihad for over seventy years. Reporters who uncovered the stories are found beheaded in the street.

The U.S. Congress convenes in a secret location for fear of more insurgent attacks on the nation's capitol building.

One-third of all the House or Representatives and several senators are Islamic worshipers, all of whom make greater demands for more recognition of the Quran as a body of law. Some milque toast politicians continue to acquiesce to radicals thinking that appeasement will work rather than any drastic measures that will preserve what is left of the U.S. government.

The core of many major cities have converted almost entirely to Islamic rule. Women are being kidnaped and raped at will because they do not cover their heads with the hijab or violate other aspects of Sharia law. Muslim youths claim it is their right. Clerics support the rapists. Bands of American civilian militia with high powered arms, including machine guns take to the streets to supplement law enforcement. Clashes escalate with Muslims and militia, leaving police overwhelmed and the National Guard impotent because their numbers have diminished because of the Irani war. Criminal courts are jammed with cases against Muslims, all of whom seem to feel they are martyrs just by going to jail for Allah. Judges have been killed. Many more have resigned.

The Mall of America in Minneapolis, Minnesota has been bombed. The Peachtree Hotel in Atlanta has been bombed. Atlanta's MARTA rail system has been bombed. Seattle's Space Needle has been bombed. Bombs have been detonated at major sporting and entertainment events. Few are held now. Major League Baseball goes bankrupt for lack of attendance at ball parks. Low attendance is also critical at NBA and NFL sporting events.

Under manned and under armed, the American military has been forced out of Iraq which is now a radical Sunni Muslim state, the so-called puppet democracy abolished. Forty years and many thousands of dead Americans accomplished nothing, in the long term. Meanwhile, fighting goes on inside of Iran, depleting our forces so critically, the Army, Navy and Marines try to recruit soldiers from the prison system. The draft has been in effect for 35 years, but the pool of qualified candidates are severely diminished because of deferments, flights to foreign countries and a large Muslim pool which now automatically disqualifies anyone from the military.

The economy is in shambles, especially after a major bombing on Wall Street and selected department buildings in Washington D.C., such as Treasury and Transportation. Interest rates are so high, there are no new home buyers. The real estate market has dried up. Ford, GM and Chrysler have crashed into bankruptcy. Millions of jobs are gone, families are starving, homeless and without medical care.

In major cities and many suburbs, Americans are awakened every morning to the call for prayer bellowing from the minaret of Islamic mosques in Arabic. This goes on five times a day, every day.

Across the ocean, at least four European nations are now predominantly Muslim with Islamic Sharia law being enforced in the streets of Paris, Amsterdam, Stockholm and Madrid. London is seen as the next to fall. Many Brits are emigrating to safe havens in foreign lands, such as Australia, New Zealand and South Africa. NATO is rendered useless.

The old problems of illegal immigration are ended and slammed in reverse. Hispanics, young and old, all over the country scramble to leave the U.S. and go back to Mexico, Cuba, and South America, no longer enthralled with the paradise of America and feeling less safe in our country than in their own.

Bookstores and libraries that house reading material unflattering to Islam are targets of terror threats, demonstrations and employee harassment. Many capitulate and remove books from the shelves, despite their truth and accuracy.

At least two major news networks have been ostensibly commandeered by Muslim radicals, with a majority of Saudis as voting members on the boards of directors. Any news that is not advantageous to the cause of Islam is aborted before it's aired. News networks that continue to report the truth, are subjected to threats of terror. One network

CEO has been found tortured and murdered, sending a grisly message to the American press. Al Jazzera, the official network for Arab news, is now based in Chicago, with affiliates in many other cities.

Conversions to the Islamic faith rise by the millions as people everywhere are in fear of being deemed an "infidel". Christian mothers are teaching their children the Quran, hoping to save their lives. Jews are fleeing anywhere they feel they can hide. In 2006, there were seven million Muslims in the United States. Now there are seventy million.

2106 — One Hundred Years From Today

Israel is gone, having been conquered by overpopulating Arab Muslims and underpopulating Jews, not to mention the detonation of one nuclear bomb in the center of Tel Aviv, killing 100,000 Israelis, tourists and Arabs and permanently injuring a half million more. Palestinians exalt in victory. A small band of Jews, perhaps a half million survivors of the New Holocaust, have dispersed and assimilated into other lands, like Russia, Australia, Brazil, South Africa and Madagascar.

All of Europe, North Africa, India and the mideast is under control of the Saudi Kingdom, including Iran, Iraq and Egypt. They are beginning to make inroads in Thailand, Sri Lanka, Siberia, New Zealand and Australia. China, Japan and some South American countries are seen as the last and most difficult bastions of the non-Muslim world to conquer.

The Islamic Republic of America has moved its center of government to the heart of Osama City, once known as Manhattan. Transportation across the East and Hudson Rivers are by bridge and boat only, because the subways no longer exist due to bombings during the jihad. Women everywhere, regardless of race, background or ethnicity, all look the same under black abayas. Other cities — which are awarded some local autonomy by the new government — are more fundamentalist Taliban and require women to wear burkas, where not even the eyes are exposed. In order to establish harmony and obedience in the new republic, Religious Police roam the streets whipping, beating and arresting people for the most minor of Islamic violations.

The American justice system has been dismantled in favor of Sharia Law. Ten million prison inmates are given a one-time opportunity to convert to Islam. Those that do not are ceremoniously beheaded because of the crimes they had committed under American law. The government said this was better than releasing mentally insane, violent criminals, drug users and potential insurgents back into the cities.

There is no more Senate, House of Representatives, Supreme Court, FBI or Department of Defense. The government buildings of Washington D.C. no longer exist, all bombed into ruin save the Capitol building which has been converted into the largest mosque in the world. Museums are gone, with artifacts and memorabilia lost to the ages. The U.S. Constitution and the Declaration of Independence is burned down along with the Library Of Congress.

All schools and colleges have been converted to Islamic Learning Centers where all children are indoctrinated in the Quran. What once were conventional history books are destroyed. As far as the Islamics are concerned, there never was a United

States, other than the great Satan which they conquered with their martyrs and warriors. In another one or two generations, there will be no legacy or knowledge of Thomas Jefferson, George Washington, Abe Lincoln, Thomas Edison, Martin Luther King Jr., Elvis Presley, Oprah, Michael Jordan, Billy Graham or Tiger Woods. Also banished to the ages, as though they never existed — not even mentioned as asterisks in Islamic history books — baseball, basketball, football, television sit-coms, Jeopardy, CNN and other non-Islamic news networks, the Grammys, Oscars, Tonys and CMA awards, because there is no more rock and roll, country music, Broadway shows and motion pictures. *Gone With the Wind*, *Schindler's List* and *King Kong*, Mozart, Beethoven, Picasso and DaVinci virtually disappear from the planet. Christmas, Easter, Thanksgiving and Halloween will be rendered null and void, not even a memory.

All currency reverts to the riyal, and the dollar is abolished. Banks are owned and operated by the government.

Cemeteries will have been ploughed over, including Arlington and the Memorial at Gettysburg. Statues and memorials, like the Marine flag raising at Mount Suribachi, Liberty in New York, and the Viet Nam and WW II memorials, Lincoln and Jefferson Memorials, no longer exist. Mount Rushmore succumbs to two tons of dynamite. Children's theme parks vanish, including Disneyworld and Six Flags over Georgia.

Those who are Jewish have either vanished into hiding or have been executed.

In smaller towns and cities, pockets of frightened Christians still remain, but hide like rats in a cave practicing their religion in crude abodes with hidden bibles and illegal shotguns, praying for the coming of a Messiah to take them from this life of misery. Children listen as elder patriarchs and matriarchs describe America as it once existed, a virtual paradise, where people were free to think, speak, worship, sing, roam, wear what they wanted, listen to music, drive cars, and buy tooth paste, beer and candy at the local market and eat hot dogs made from pork. The children also learn how a corrupt government virtually gave the country away.

Slavery is legalized. Hard-nosed whites, Hispanics and blacks who refused to convert and follow the daily life of a devout Muslim, and in good health, are relegated to working the farms and factories in exchange for life, food and a squaller's hut. Millions of young girls vanish from schools, destined for a slave's life either as a wife, concubine or a sex object until she is killed like a useless dog.

For those few remaining non-Muslims who desperately cling to a heritage, they are the last vestige of ancestry, for their children, and their children's children will never know that their great-grandparents were once musical geniuses, war heros, doctors, firemen, artists, watchmakers, religious icons or political leaders. There will be no scrapbooks, no mementos, no photographs and videos to see the paradise that once was. And they will ask, "What happened?"

2206 — Two Hundred Years From Today

What once were ambers waves of grain and purple mountain majesties above the fruited plain, is now a vast desert wasteland. Cities that once bustled with life, prosperity and constant movement are now giant ghost towns made of concrete canyons, pot-holed streets, rusted automobiles and buses, broken glass everywhere and crumbled skyscrapers.

The world's supply of crude oil has — for the most part — dried up. What oil fields are left, cannot be harvested because the machinery and manpower no longer is available or operable. Even if oil could be retrieved and refined, there are few, if any, vehicles, planes, trains and ships in regular operation to warrant the effort.

Onslaughts of hurricanes, tornadoes, tsunamis, earthquakes and volcanic eruptions, have contributed to famine and disease across the land where there are no medical facilities that can meet the demand for treatment. Millions die, and are left in the fields and roads to rot.

Wandering tribes of mixed-race humans fight for survival by killing animals and eating off the vine, much the same as Cro-Magnon did 20,000 years ago. There are no televisions, no newspapers, no mass communications of any kind. Music comes from the voice of humans, because there are no violins, no pianos, no guitars and trumpets. What we think of as homes, are now make-shift shanty huts, tree houses, abandoned buildings and caves. But, there are mosques, and prayer five times a day. Families consist of mothers and children who cling to one another while the father seeks food and shelter, and if lucky, an item of clothing. If anything good has come from it all, the rate of divorce has dropped and few homes are fatherless any more. There is simply no where for them to go.

Mortality rates are astronomical, one of every two babies born do not survive past six months of age.

The elderly rarely live past the age of sixty, especially those with debilitating diseases. Diabetes, Cancer, Parkinson's and other diseases, once treatable, are a virtual death sentence. Many prefer death to life and ask to be euthanized. There is no definition of "happy," because the emotion is not pertinent.

Society under Islam has virtually regressed back to the seventh century mode of living.

Amazingly, one young boy digging dirt in a deserted corn field in what once was known as Iowa, finds a small rectangular box wrapped in plastic, with a title written in bold, black letters, *"Planet of the Apes."*

It all could have been averted with a smidgen of foresight and government integrity. Unfortunately, none existed.

"Individual Moslems may show splendid qualities but the influence of the religion paralyzes the social development of those who follow it. No stronger retrograde force exists in the world. Far from being moribund, Mohammedanism is a militant and proselytizing faith. It has already spread throughout Central Africa, raising fearless warriors at every step; and were it not that Christianity is sheltered in the strong arms of science, the science against which it had vainly struggled, the civilization of modern Europe might fall, as fell the civilization of ancient Rome."

— Sir Winston Churchill, from *The River War*, First edition, 1899.

CHAPTER FIFTEEN

CHANGING THE COURSE

The most important question: What can we do? And when?

The time, is now. But we must all be ready to make sacrifices. They are but a small investment in order to preserve the future of America for the ensuing generations. We tend to be a short-sighted society. Americans rarely think in these terms, because we are bogged down in routine, studying stocks and bonds, commuting to jobs, watching television, listening to rock music, playing with kids, serving ribs at the church barbeque, shopping at Wal-mart and basically caring only about today and the hell with tomorrow. We think about war in the abstract, as a news event in a foreign land, not something that slams us in the face with the smell of blood and guts every day like it did the victims of Europe in WW II.

Here are fourteen points which, in my view, are essential for altering the course of certain tragedy for our children and grandchildren.

Truth In Media

The national media must rise to the occasion. The freedom of press is in jeopardy if the jihadists ever have their way. Journalists and staffers in the media are certainly aware of the undercurrents that prevail, more so even than the government because they are not shackled by politically correct edicts and bureaucratic restraints. While the nightly news focuses on terror attacks in Iraq, they spend little precious air time exposing Wahhabi Islam in the U.S., its goals to conquer and its impact on our government. Because the invasion is subtle, it does not make sensational news.

Media saturation and exposure of this threat is paramount. Fox News' Bill O'Reilly is one of the few commentators who was willing to stand up to an Islamic menace on national television by confronting Sami Al Arian. Cal Thomas is among a handful of journalists who has consistently spoken out on this subject. There are few others. Three major networks, three cable channels and hundreds of major newspapers dispatch reporters for stories around the globe, yet we hear little about the Wahhabi cancer spreading inside our shores. They spend too little time and effort informing the American people of what influences the Saudi regime is exerting over our government, and what the future portends if we don't put a stop to it. The information is certainly out there.

News magazine shows such as *60 Minutes*, *Dateline*, *20/20* and others should seek out authors like Paul Sperry and Robert Spencer and have them expose the Saudi problem on national television. The U.S. Congress, as well, should lend an ear to such valid sources of information. More media reps should infiltrate the Wahhabi mosques and ask questions about money laundering, financing terror, harboring murderers, and using religion as subterfuge for conducting espionage and waging a non-shooting war. Sure, they will claim "discrimination" and "religious bias", but so what.

Journalists should be pinning FBI Director Robert Mueller against the wall asking why Jewish translators were categorically excluded from employment in the Bureau in deference to Arabs. Why did a Muslim agent get away with refusing to wear a wire against a fellow Muslim? Why haven't Muslim translators who refuse to interpret been fired or prosecuted? Why did the FBI hire Arab translators that were sympathetic to the perpetrators of 9/11?

Transportation Secretary Norman Mineta should be answering questions for the American public, explaining why the airport security search little old ladies from North Dakota, but not Islamic young men from Yemen. When 99 percent of all terrorist acts are committed by Islamic fundamentalists, why are we not profiling?

Like O'Reilly, journalists in all four corners of the nation should be posing tougher questions to clerics and other Muslim leaders who are known to support the overthrow of our government, and the extinction of Israel as a nation.

The Bush administration should be queried hard about their bosom relationship with Wahhabi Saudis, and why they continue to receive such premier treatment, especially the days after 9/11. The Bush people should be asked if they are even aware of the objectives of Wahhabi Islamics, that they are determined to bring down our government through infiltration of our infrastructure. Ask Mr.

Bush, "How can you claim to be fighting terror, when the financiers of terror and international jihad are among your most protected friends?"

If ever there was a time we needed a press with guts, it's now. In the aftermath of the Denmark cartoons which spawned Muslim rioting around the world, many newspaper editorials flirted with condemning the Danish publication for printing the cartoon, saying it was insensitive to Muslims and that they had a right to be upset. That's not guts. That's fear. While no newspaper condoned the violence that ensued, the message was clear that sympathies were afforded Muslims. Capitulation to the threat of violence will only beget more violence.

The press also must realize that they are being used as tools of the jihadists, often playing into their hands. While there is a fine line between the right to report news and aiding in the cause of terror, it is usually resolved in favor of a free press. But the press should be aware that those who routinely protest and commit dastardly deeds wouldn't come out of the door if it were not for the omnipresence of cameras.

Wean Off The Mid-east Oil Teat

It is essential that we — and the European union — become oil independent and tell the Saudis to go pound sand. They certainly have plenty of that. Since the early part of the twentieth century, we have allowed ourselves to fall hostage to third-world nations who are determined to have us all to live a seventh century world. The stupidity continues because of politics, worries over inflation and maintaining the status quo with OPEC.

Anyone who has every read a newspaper knows

that the technology is out there. The government certainly knows it's out there. Hydrogen fuel cells, solar power, coal, shale, ethanol and electricity are all in development and/or available today. We can do it, but we don't. We stay mired in Saudi up-manship. Plus, crude oil in huge reserves are buried in nations much more compatible and friendly to the United States, such as Canada and Mexico and South America. Canada is the ninth largest producer of crude oil in the world, and they have huge un-tapped deposits that may actually exceed the potential of the mid-east. While we import heavily from Canada and Mexico today, those imports can be stepped up if the demand was there and we had the guts to break with the mid-east.

To their credit, Ford and General Motors have teamed up with energy companies on projects that could make E85 — ethanol — a mainstream fuel. E85 is a blend of 85 percent alcohol made from mid-west corn, and 15 percent gasoline. The president conceded in his State of the Union speech on January of 2006, that ethanol fuels can make our dependence on mid-east oil a thing of the past. Now is the time to put money where the mouth is, and put the power of the U.S. government in motion to accelerate the program. If the country of Brazil can do it, we can.

I believe in conserving the natural environment, but sometimes we must weigh priorities. It is more critical that we break from this strangle-hold than to worry about drilling and laying a pipeline across Alaska. If the oil is there, let's go for it, and tell the sheiks bye-bye.

When the electric light bulb came into being, we didn't stay with the gaslight because the manufacturers of gaslights would go bankrupt. We moved on. The government did what was best for Americans, not best for the corporations. Likewise, the government must play hardball with major corporations that refine oil and manufacture automobile and airplane engines, and propel us into the 21st century building modernized engines.

If all this came to fruition, we may see a spike in the cost of living, but that is necessary in order to reach the goal of political and economic independence. We'll see more hybrids and four cylinder cars on the road, than SUVs and motor homes. The price of an airline ticket will go up. And we'll not take as many long road trips as we did before. It would all be temporary until final independence is reached, and we are no longer threatened by the influence of Wahhabism. Sometimes, we must make tough choices.

Vote Smart

Recent presidential elections have been, for many, a matter of choosing the better of bad choices as opposed to electing great leaders. We must elect representatives who truly serve the best interest of the people, and not driven by the almighty dollar and the quest for power.

One example of voters who fail to check out a candidate, are the citizens of Georgia's 4th congressional district. That seat is held by Representative Cynthia McKinney. Here's a partial list of McKinney's most prominent donors:

Hani Y. Awadallah, Arab American Civic Organization.

Jesse Aweida, founder, American Task Force on Palestine.

Belal Dalati, vice president of Arab-American Broadcasting Co.

Yaser Elmenshawy, chairman, Islamic Council of New Jersey.

Rafeeq Jaber, president, Islamic Association for Palestine, an offshoot of Hamas.

Oussama Jammal, president, Bridgeview Mosque.

Faroque Khan, president, Islamic Center of Long Island.

Mahmoud A Nimer, director, Islamic Academy of Florida (established by Sami al Arian).

Talat Othman, chairman, Islamic Free Market Institute.

Khalid Qazi, American Muslim Council of western New York.

Allam Reheem, former director, Islamic Academy of Florida.

Talal Sunbulli, former chairman, Council of Islamic Organizations of Chicago.

There are many more.

Does anyone doubt where her loyalties lie?

Americans often elect people for the wrong reasons. George W. Bush managed to suck ten million voters over to the Republican side the moment he publically announced he was influenced most in his life by Jesus Christ. It was a successful ploy to nail down a giant voting block in one package. Titillated Christian fundamentalists saw this as an opportunity to elect one of their own, and it mattered not if he'd sell out the country for oil, profits and corporate favors. Blinded by passion, the fundamentalists got what they wanted, and Bush got what he wanted. The hell with the rest of us.

Single-issue voting can be very dangerous.

Millions of voters wear blinders when it comes to hot button issues like abortion and prayer in school which can help to elect the wrong person for the wrong reasons.

The corrupt two-party system limits us to injurious candidates such as George W. Bush and John Kerry where influence and power is wielded by corporations and lobbyists in exchange for favors once their man (or woman) sits in the Oval Office. Those favors are paid back at the expense of the American taxpayer. Whether it's legal or not, the system is unarguably corrupt and dishonest.

The best of all scenarios would be a third party, or independent candidate who is incorruptible and willing to stand up to negative influences within our land without concern of political correctness. Ross Perot was such a candidate back in 1992, wealthy, smart, gutsy and inapproachable by the forces of greed. Whether we elect a libertarian, a Green Party member, or an independent, it is vitally important that the voters send a message to the two major parties: No more corruption.

We must elect a president who does what's best for Americans, not illegal aliens, not corporate profiteers, not oil conglomerates, not some voting block and not the squeaky wheel.

Unify With The Free World

We must convince the international community to recognize and act upon the ominous threat to the future of world peace by militant Islam. Once no longer deemed a peaceful religion but a forceful and declared enemy, we can join hands in stemming the tide and put a stop to the advance of international jihad. We need unity. The enemy works hard at creating divisiveness, and they succeed. Why do we allow ourselves to fall into their hands?

Our relationship with foreign nations are at an all-time low. The populace of our most diligent allies often see us as arrogant international bullies. Millions of Muslims — in general — hate us, but that's normal because they are brainwashed so from birth. We will not survive unless we have the backing of our allies throughout the world, particularly in Europe, Russia, Japan and Australia. The leadership of all these nations should establish a close dialogue regarding one issue: World peace in the face of militant Islam. At the top of the list, stem the tide of immigration from nations hostile to the free world and step up deportation of those who would overthrow the existing governments. All nations should stand up to the militant Islamic world and declare: "We accept any and all religions that are peaceful and tolerant. Any religious faction that declares/supports holy war against the peace loving people of the world, will be considered a warring enemy and dealt with accordingly."

Where is that man who said, "When the going gets tough, the tough get going?"

Declare War

First, the government must officially define "Militant Islam" as a non-religion, but a fascist form of government and a sworn enemy of the U.S. and the free world in general. Defined, "Militant Islam" is that faction of the Muslim religion that engages in activities, or the support of activities, designed to overthrow the government of the United States.

Emphasis on support of activities.

Support of such activities includes, but is not limited to: financial aid, conspiracy to aid and abet, planning and directing subversive activities, harboring and assisting those who carry out acts of terror, and etc. The message must ring true. Militant Islam no longer has an unlimited license to openly practice jihad inside the borders of this country.

With a declaration of war, mosques and Islamic learning centers that plot, harbor, finance, and support jihad can be targeted as subversive organizations hiding under a guise of religious freedom, and thereby closed down and/or lose their standing as tax-exempt religious institutions.

A declaration of war will also enable the U.S. to restrict the flow of anti-American propaganda by enemy agents inside colleges, prisons and other institutions where militants are prime for recruitment.

With a declaration of war, we can restrict immigration to persons from nations that are in support of international jihad. That includes placing a ban on student visas for persons from countries like Saudi Arabia, Syria, Iran and the Palestinian front. Yes, that's discriminating. I see it differently than many leftists. The United States is my country, not some mid-east mullah's. We Americans have contributed toward making this a great and secure nation, they haven't. They haven't the right to tear it down.

A declaration of war will pave the way for easy deportation of Islamic aliens — legal and illegal — who are proponents of jihad.

And the declaration of war will provide law enforcement and our counter-intelligence forces more clout in tapping into the enemy wall of secrecy.

Appeal To Moderate Muslims

Truly peaceful Muslims who reject the concept of jihad and world domination must speak out and consider breaking from the militant sect by establishing a new order of Islam They should denounce all forms of violence and hatred, and strive toward living in harmony among people of other religions. The great divide is basically attributed to the Quran's edicts about intolerance toward non-believers, i.e. non-Muslims.

I am certain that peaceful Muslims exist throughout the world who are not radical and only wish to practice their faith in a more modernized manner. But they are intimidated by the radical practitioners who insist that all non-Muslims of the world are infidels. As long as that remains in the teachings of Islam, there will never be peace.

The greatest force toward establishing world peace would be a Muslim uprising against militant jihad, against violence and against hatred. They must earnestly promote tolerance of all peoples, including Christians, Buddhists, atheists, homosexuals, Gypsies, blacks, whites, Spanish, French, English, Asian and, of course, Jews. Muslims who wish to practice their faith must be afforded that freedom, providing they do not support jihad or war in any fashion. Muslims who proclaim jihad, or support the overthrow of the U.S. government should be disassociated from religious status and identified as an enemy of the people.

For Islam to truly be a religion of peace, Muslims should renounce those parts of the Quran which endorse hatred and violence toward others, and accept people who do not believe as they do — not as an enemy, but as human beings who coexist on the same planet. It would be wonderful for all peace-loving Muslims if a great and charismatic leader emerged who could help his people to see the light, and initiate change. What is needed, perhaps, is a new testament for the Quran, one that teaches love for all, and one that can be adapted to modern times, not ancient Arabia when head-chopping and wife-slavery were the tenets of the day.

We need to hear more from former Muslims as well, but few will ever be speaking out because of the fear factor. Delegates of the religion of peace are well known for murdering those who have re-nounced Islam and then dare to make their views known.

Few have displayed the courage of Doctor Wafa Sultan, a Syrian-born psychologist from California, who — in February of 2006 — was interviewed on Al Jazeera television when she shocked the host by bitterly criticizing Muslim clerics, holy warriors and political leaders who, she says, have distorted the teachings of Muhammad and the Quran for fourteen centuries. To the dismay of Islamic radicals everywhere, excerpts of her interview have piqued the interest of millions around the world via the internet.

"Only the Muslims defend their beliefs by burning down churches, killing people and destroying embassies," she said. *"This path will not yield any results. The Muslims must ask themselves what they can to for humankind before they demand that humankind respect them."*

Her most poignant remarks proved the most vexing to the interviewer. *"We have not seen a single*

Jew blow himself up in a German restaurant. We have not seen a single Jew destroy a church. We have not seen a single Jew protest by killing people." Speaking of the Holocaust, she said, *"The Jews have come from tragedy and forced the world to respect them with their knowledge, not with their terror; with their work, not with their crying and yelling."*

The *New York Times* reported in March, 2006, that her telephone answering machine has been filled with threats and promises of reprisal. But Islamic reformers have praised her for saying out loud, in Arabic and on the most widely seen television network in the Arab world, what few Muslims dare to say even in private.

The peaceful free world craves for the emergence of more Wafa Sultan's, much the same as the American Negro craved the emergence of a Martin Luther King, Jr in the 1950's. It's time, now, that those Islamic reformers that privately praise Doctor Sultan come out of hiding en masse, as progressives and humanitarians, and begin standing up for the goodness that Islam embraces and denounce the hatred that it espouses.

Where are you, Kareem Abdul Jabbar? Muhammad Ali? Where are your children, your brothers and your peers who reject the militant form of Islam and truly wish for harmony among us all?

Professor Ali Manai said it best when he wrote: *"No amount of military action will rid the world of Islamic militants. The swamp that must be drained is not in the mountains of Afghanistan, but in the minds of hundreds of millions of Muslims. It is time for a new synthesis in Islam, and it can only be done from within by enlightened, informed and faithful Muslims."*

Stem Immigration

Illegal immigration must be halted and legal immigration monitored more closely. This humongous problem has mushroomed out of control since Mr. Bush has been in office. The administration's soft approach toward illegals from Mexico has opened the door to terrorists from all sides of the planet. It is nothing more than pay-back politics, as the Bush crowd extends appreciation to the agriculture and hotel/motel lobbies for their support in getting him elected. In turn, the administration does all it can to ensure these lobbies employ mass labor at low cost, for high profits. It has nothing to do with humanitarian motives.

While there are many other problems created by illegal immigration, nothing is more critical than the infiltration of enemy forces, thousands of whom are known to have crossed over the Mexican border, leaving copies of the Quran and prayer rugs behind. Terror training camps have been identified inside Mexico. Members of al Qaeda have been known to study Spanish and pose as Mexicans coming into the country. Loopholes for Mexicans are the same loopholes for Iranis, Syrians and Pakistanis.

Laws must be changed that legitimize illegal aliens once they bear a child on American soil. Millions of women and children have become burdens to the American taxpayer for life, because they managed to give birth after they crossed the border.

The U.S. must start prosecuting employers who knowingly hire illegals. Once the well is dry, the crossings will diminish. As this book is written, a bill in congress is pending that would further criminalize illegal crossings and hold those accountable who employ illegals as law breakers. While thousands of illegals and their sympathizers protest this bill, most Americans hope and pray that the politicians will hold fast and not buckle under to pressure. Most important, is to secure our borders from enemy infiltration.

We must also deport or prosecute all foreigners who actively conspire, aid or support the overthrow of the U.S. government. Legal or not, the message should ring loud and clear: Enemy agents are not welcome here. If a Saudi cleric wants to conspire against the U.S., let him do it in Rihyad or Damascus.

Tighten Education Standards

States must adopt minimum standards for all of child education, which includes learning the history, geography and government of the U.S., putting a stop to jihad indoctrination inside Islamic learning centers.

In most states, parents who home-school their children are required to adhere to minimum standards of education. Those children must pass tests demonstrating knowledge of American presidents, national milestones, literature, music, government, English, math and science. Kids in public schools recite a pledge of allegiance to the Unites States, with or without "Under God" in the text. A loyalty to the nation is developed among children in order to form a harmonious society, while still bending to the freedoms provided in the Bill of Rights. While we are admiring and tolerant of other cultures, we should be instilling American culture and values into children as well. If our kids attended school in France, Germany or Japan, they'd become immersed in their respective cultures.

Religious schools, be they Christian, Jewish or Muslim, should also be held to standards which show they have acquired these minimum standards of learning. Mosques and learning centers that object or fail to comply, and instead, drill nothing other than the Quran into the brains of kids, should lose their license and status as a school. With the declaration of war in effect, those mosques and learning centers that preach hate, prejudice, jihad and martyrism can be closed.

The message: Like Christians, Jews, Buddhists and atheists, Muslim children who live and go to school in the United States must learn the basics about America and its history, and assimilate as Americans.

It's too bad American leaders don't have the guts to lead as do the Australians. That country's Minister of Education, Brendan Nelson made his point clearly in August of 2005 when he publicly told Muslims in Australia, *"We believe in giving every person a fair go, we don't care where people come from, we don't mind what religion they've got. But what we want them to do is commit to the Australian constitution, Australian rule of law and basically, people who don't want to be Australians, and they don't want to live by Australian values and understand them, well, they can basically clear off."*

According to *The World Today*, Doctor Nelson and Prime Minister John Howard has met with the Australian Federation of Islamic councils to discuss programs that ensure students understand Australia's history, culture and values. Muslim leaders there have voiced their agreement to the will of the Australian government, that they all will respect the democratic institutions and practices of the country where they live. Prime Minister Howard and his cabinet made it clear that their government would not tolerate Muslim radicals creating havoc in their country and that any Muslim who wanted to live under Sharia law should get out of the country.

Imagine that coming from the mouth of an American politician?

Amend The Constitution

Lawmakers should pass a constitutional amendment (or act of congress) as it pertains to the freedom of religion, altering the language to read: "...freedom of religion providing religious institutions are not falsely used as subterfuge by an enemy intent on overthrowing the government." The reasons are obvious.

Restrict Foreign Investments

With a declaration of war, the United States can ban foreign investments by those who directly or indirectly support jihad, and seize all funds. Owning businesses and property in the United States, is like owning part of America. Those who wish to see America destroyed, cannot be permitted a foot in that door.

Decriminalize Drugs

We must legalize some illicit drugs in order to stem the flow of monies to al Qaeda and other militant Islamics, thus freeing law enforcement to center more on subversive activities amid our enemies. The Spanish and Dutch have implemented some of this with much success. This would also help to deplete the inmate population of prisons from non-violent offenders who have formed anti-American sentiments, and are prime targets for militant Islamic recruitment.

Legalization of heroin, for example, would dry up the black market which is now thriving at an all-time high, beginning with the poppy fields in Afghanistan which al Qaeda depends on for stocking munitions and armament. There are approximately one million heroin addicts in the Unites States, and another two million or more in Europe, most of whom are contributing to the cause of terrorism. By legalizing, we can declare addiction as a disease, and start treating people accordingly. Those who are confirmed addicts can receive free heroin at licensed clinics, thereby relieving them of the need to deal, sell and to make street buys. The pusher would become obsolete. And desperate addicts would no longer have to resort to violence and property crimes to support their habit. People would be safer, drug cartels would vanish and the terrorists would have to seek new sources for funding. This is what the Swiss has done and trafficking has all but vanished.

Same goes for legalizing marijuana. It's plain stupid that the United States has nearly twenty million people who are users of pot, but we still deem it a crime and jam our jails with harmless human beings. All law enforcement money and energy that goes into the lost war on drugs, can be redirected toward fighting a true enemy that endangers Americans far more than marijuana. And by legalizing, we can harness billions in tax revenue, rather than continuing to squander billions of taxpayer funds on a losing cause.

Be Tough

We should put Saudi Arabia and other Muslim extremist countries on notice that any terrorist attack by insurgents from their nation on our soil will be considered an act of war, and we will reserve the right to retaliate with whatever force we deem is necessary to prevent any further attacks on our citizens. If the Saudis know we are ready to obliterate Riyhad if another 9/11 occurs, you can bet they will be making deals around the Islamic world to save their barbaric butts. Same with Iran, Syria, Yemen and Pakistan.

We have to show we mean business. There is no such thing as negotiating with an enemy who is driven by Allah's message to kill us all. We cannot allow ourselves to be blind-sided again. And it is the duty of our government representatives, starting with the president, to do everything within their power to forestall another act of terror against our people, even if it means pissing off the Saudis.

No, I'm not holding my breath.

End Political Correctness

Start profiling. Let's face reality, human beings do it anyway whether we admit it or not. But it's time the government step up and do what's necessary and not always what is politically correct. Some folks will think this comes across as racist, but it's a risk worth taking. It is imperative that we discriminate when lives are in danger and the nation is in peril.

As a cop, I investigated many cases where the profile of a criminal aided in apprehension and/or putting a stop to criminal behavior. For example, when we knew that a series of killings were perpetrated by a blond-haired male wearing glasses, the police searched for men fitting that profile. Sure many blond-haired, bespectacled men were pulled over, checked out and sent on their way, but eventually the killer was caught because of descriptive profiling. That's life. No apologies when innocent lives are in danger.

Our nation is being victimized by criminals who have harmed us greatly, who threaten to harm us again, and will undoubtedly succeed. No decent American wants to discriminate against a race or ethnic group, but facts are facts. Those who carry out terrorist acts are mostly young mid-east or North African Muslim men (and a very few women) who are the product of brainwashing from birth, made to believe that their moment of glory and everlasting life with virgins at their feet, is the day they die as martyrs for Allah. The older men and clerics do the financing, preaching and spiritual support. The women perform their "duties", servicing men as they are told. Muslim mothers proudly prepare their suicide-ready sons for their day of glory, as though they are going off to a graduation.

It is plain idiocy that we do not profile. It is plain idiocy that we adhere to political correctness in deference to common sense, and the safety of our citizens.

I would dare Mr. Bush or any other politician, journalist or American citizen to tell me they would not feel uneasy boarding an airplane when they see that same plane has been boarded by a young mid-east males, seemingly Arab, Irani, Pakistani and all Muslim. While the overwhelming majority of mid-eastern people are non-threatening, they are also fully aware that the carnage that is ravaging the planet, from the United States, to Europe and Asia, is born of Islamic hatred spawned from those regions. Unfortunately, like those blond-haired men in my serial-killer scenario, innocent mid-easterners must bite that bullet and accept that some of their ethnic peers have brought on the necessary scourge of discrimination.

Journalist Ann Coulter said it best. *"The Bush administration's obstinate refusal to profile Middle Easterners has been the one massive gaping hole in national security since the 9/11 attacks."*

In her column of February 2nd, 2006, dead-on reporter Michelle Malkin told us that on the Tuesday afternoon in advance of the State of the Union address, the Council on American-Islamic Relations (CAIR) issued an ultimatum warning President Bush to "avoid the use of hot-button terms such as 'Islamofascism,' 'militant jihadism,' 'Islamic radicalism' or 'totalitarian Islamic empire'" in his speech — in other words, advising Bush not to identify our enemies for the sake of tolerance and diversity.

Guess what...

Public Outrage

Serious issues and problems of the world, i.e.,

the Iraq war, immigration, hurricanes, racial unrest, terrorism, etc., take up 99 percent of the information flow from the media, therefore we hear little about the ominous threat of the Wahhabi infiltration. It doesn't make spectacular news. It's not spectacular now, but it will be.

There must be a public outcry. The people of the United States are invested with power, and they should use it. In order to do that, Americans must become better educated and aware of all these happenings. Once people realize the exigency, alarm and outrage will follow.

There is no greater example of the power of the people than the outcome of the Dubai Ports fiasco. Americans are getting fed up with terrorism and deceit emanating from mid-east Muslim countries. When the Dubai ports deal became public, thanks to syndicated columnist Frank Gaffney, an avalanche of outrage swamped every senator, congressperson and governor from California to New York. Staunch republicans who usually fell in line behind the president on issues, bolted on this one, all because of the voice of the people. We can make a difference.

The enemy thrives on our ignorance. While the enemy espouses the mantra that they are a peaceful and tolerance religion, the government administration falls lockstep into the same old prop-aganda for political expediency. Americans sit around reading newspapers and watching network news, thinking we know all we need to know, allowing ourselves to be fed the politically correct version of Islamofascism by a skiddish media. Very few of us reach out for more truth and objective sources of information. I was just as guilty before 9/11.

When I speak at libraries, churches and other civic organizations I am stunned to learn just how uninformed we are as a people in jeopardy. When asking folks if they've read up on the Quran, or the history of Islam, or Muhammad, or the plight of Islamic jihad, rarely a hand is raised. People have heard about terrorists, and al Qaeda, and that's all they need to know.

It is not enough to settle for television sound bites and blurbs edited in newspapers. Our outcry must be directed, not just at terrorists, but the more sinister insurgency that is ballooning inside the United States. Complacency is the forebearer of doom. It is what the enemy is counting on.

Christian fundamentalists, in particular, must wake up to the reality that they — like Jews — are on the target list for extinction once the militant Islamics have their way. They have been betrayed by this president many times over, as he cunningly gave the impression of fighting a war on terror, when in fact, he has been capitulating to a covert enemy inside our borders since the day he took office. Outrage is needed from the nation's Christians.

Public outcry can stir government leaders into meaningful action. Demonstrations, newspaper articles, letters to congressmen, media engagement and the election of honest representatives are but a few measures that may be effective in stemming the tide of Islamofascist jihad. While we can embrace truly peaceful Muslims, as we do other religions, we must show intolerence to those Islamic entities that support the overthrow of the U.S. government.

Let's hope it's not too late.

WE HAVE BEEN WARNED

The following is a speech (excerpted) delivered by Ms. Brigitte Gabriel at the Intelligence Summit in Washington DC, Saturday, February 18, 2006. Ms. Gabriel is a former news anchor of World News for Middle East television and founder of the American Congress For Truth. She is widely considered an expert in middle eastern affairs.

"The most important element of intelligence has to be understanding the mind-set and intention of the enemy. The West has been wallowing in a state of ignorance and denial for thirty years as Muslim extremist perpetrated evil against innocent victims in the name of Allah.

"I was ten years old when my home exploded around me, burying me under the rubble and leaving me to drink my blood to survive, as the perpetrators shouted "Allah Akbar!" My only crime was that I was a Christian living in a Christian town. At 10 years old, I learned the meaning of the word infidel.

"I had a crash course in survival. Not in the Girl Scouts, but in a bomb shelter where I lived for seven

years in pitch darkness, freezing cold, drinking stale water and eating grass to live.

"As a victim of Islamic terror, I was amazed when I saw Americans waking up on September 12, 2001, and asking themselves ,'Why do they hate us?" The psychoanalyst experts were coming up with all sort of excuses as to what did we do to offend the Muslim World. But if America and the West were paying attention to the Middle East they would not have had to ask the question. Simply put, they hate us because we are defined in their eyes by one simple word: Infidels

"America and the West are doomed to failure in this war unless they stand up and identify the real enemy: Islam. You hear about Wahabbi and Salafi Islam as the only extreme form of Islam. All the other Muslims, supposedly, are wonderful moderates. Closer to the truth are the pictures of the irrational eruption of violence in reaction to the cartoons of Mohammed printed by a Danish newspaper. From burning embassies, to calls to butcher those who mock Islam, to warnings that the West be prepared for another holocaust, those pictures have given us a glimpse into the real face of the enemy. News pictures and video of these events represent a canvas of hate decorated by different nationalities who share one common ideology of hate, bigotry and intolerance derived from one source: Authentic Islam. Islam that is awakening from centuries of slumber to reignite its wrath against the infidel and dominate the world. An Islam which has declared Intifada on the West.

"America and the West can no longer afford to lay in their lazy state of overweight ignorance. The consequences of this mental disease are starting to attack the body, and if they don't take the necessary steps now to control it, death will be knocking soon. If you want to understand the nature of the enemy we face, visualize a tapestry of snakes. They slither and they hiss, and they would eat each other alive, but they will unite in a hideous mass to achieve their common goal of imposing Islam on the world.

"We are fighting a powerful ideology that is capable of altering basic human instincts. An ideology that can turn a mother into a launching pad of death. A perfect example is a recently elected Hamas official in the Palestinian Territories who raves in heavenly joy about sending her three sons to death and offering the ones who are still alive for the cause. It is an ideology that is capable of offering highly educated individuals such as doctors and lawyers far more joy in attaining death than any respect and stature, life in society is ever capable of giving them.

"The United States has been a prime target for radical Islamic hatred and terror. Every Friday, mosques in the Middle East ring with shrill prayers and monotonous chants calling death, destruction and damnation down on America and its people.

"Even the Nazis did not turn their own children into human bombs, and then rejoice at their deaths as well the deaths of their victims.

"America cannot effectively defend itself in this war unless and until the American people understand the nature of the enemy that we face. Even after 9/11 there are those who say that we must engage our terrorist enemies, that we must 'address their grievances.' Their grievance is our freedom of religion. Their grievance is our freedom *of speech. Their grievance is our democratic process where the rule of law comes from the voices of many not that of just one prophet.*

"*Our mediocre attitude of not confronting Islamic forces of bigotry and hatred wherever they raised their ugly head in the last 30 years, has empowered and strengthened our enemy to launch a full scale attack on the very freedoms we cherish in their effort to impose their values and way of life on our civilization.*

"*If we don't wake up and challenge our Muslim community to take action against the terrorists within it, if we don't believe in ourselves as Americans and in the standards we should hold every patriotic American to, we are going to pay a price for our delusion. For the sake of our children and our country, we must wake up and take action. In the face of a torrent of hateful invective and terrorist murder, America's learning curve since the Iran hostage crisis is so shallow that it is almost flat. The longer we lay supine, the more difficult it will be to stand erect.*"

Amen.